ADVANCE REVIEWS

"Tara L. Masih has assembled a stunning colle____ ____ ____ ____ ____ of cultural diversity and personal compl____ ____ ____ ____ into this slim, beautiful volume is staggering ar____ ____ ____ ____ ____.er collection out there. These now-Am____ica____ ____ ____elers experience the intercultural er____ ____ ____ ____ ,erseas, within their own communities, ____ ____ ____ ____ ____ he voices range from adult journalists and Pe____ ____ ____ .nteers to the children of Nazis and refugees. For s____ ____ ____ ____ Third Culture Kids and the children of survivors, their h____ ____ies and true identities are hidden, and it is through engaging with food and spirituality, photographs and music, family stories and private letters, global and personal history, that they are able to recover and share the nuances of life in our globalizing planet. Each story is a polished, multifaceted gem of unprecedented color and clarity, which together form a glittering necklace that redefines what it is to be intercultural—that is, human—in the world today. This is a book I will be teaching and recommending to friends and strangers again and again."

—**Faith Adiele**, editor of *Coming of Age Around the World: A Multicultural Anthology* and author of *Meeting Faith: The Thai Forest Journals of a Black Buddhist Nun*

"In this present tumultuous age, as the peoples of the world struggle toward a sense of their individuated selves—trying to define who is their own and who is the "other"—*Chalk Circle* is a truly important book. Here we can understand that we are all one in our shared humanity."

—**Robert Olen Butler,** Pulitzer Prize Winner and recipient of the Tu Do Chinh Kien Award

"We are currently living in a time when students from myriad cultural backgrounds are becoming prominent in educational institutions in the United States. These students bring with them rich cultural experiences that are often lost as they feel compelled to assimilate into American society. Tara Masih has provided a microphone for these students to project their voices, to affirm and validate their experiences by telling their own stories. . . . This collection of essays provides a lens into intercultural experiences that will offer important insights for teachers as well as students. . . . and can spark discussions that lead to a greater understanding of and appreciation for our global community." **—Dr. Zaline M. Roy-Campbell**, Coordinator of the Program in Teaching English Language Learners, Syracuse University

"Masih has assembled an intelligent and eloquent collection of essays touching upon the complexities of intercultural relations. This book provides plenty of food for thought (fried locusts, anyone?) and fodder for meaningful classroom discussion, but there is much to engage the casual reader as well—a journey to Japan, the subtext of a song, art that burns, the confusion of being a Third Culture Kid, and much more. As soon as I reached the last page, I wanted to read it again." **—Suzanne Kamata**, editor of *Call Me Okasaan: Adventures in Multicultural Mothering* and author of *Losing Kei*

"Places are best soaked in through the tongue," Grigg-Saito writes in her essay. It is true—local markets define a place—but so do these fine stories that also come from the tongue. These mixed and multicultural writers are at work in *The Chalk Circle*, telling their stories, each in their own voice, finding, as Wright says, "the place where the rainbow gets its color." **—Diane Glancy**, editor of *Two Worlds Walking* and author of *The Dream of a Broken Field*

"Refugee students coming to . . . American resettlement cities have encountered incredible danger and deprivation to arrive. Once they arrive the struggle continues to find good jobs and housing, face down bigotry, and keep the family intact. [T]here are few texts to help them articulate and transcend their experiences. This contemporary collection of essays will be an invaluable resource. I'm especially impressed by the range of themes. . . ." **—Mary McLaughlin Slechta**, ESL instructor and author, Nottingham High School

THE CHALK CIRCLE

Intercultural Prizewinning Essays

TARA L. MASIH, Ed.

The Chalk Circle: Intercultural Prizewinning Essays

Edited by Tara L. Masih

©2012 Tara L. Masih.

ISBN: 978-1-936214-71-6

Library of Congress Control Number: 2011944309

Wyatt-MacKenzie Publishing
DEADWOOD, OREGON

Wyatt-MacKenzie Publishing, Inc, Deadwood, Oregon
www.WyattMacKenzie.com

Publisher's Cataloging-in-Publication data

Masih, Tara L.
   The chalk circle : intercultural prizewinning essays / edited by Tara L. Masih.
   p. cm.
   Includes bibliographical references and index.
   ISBN 978-1-936214-71-6

1. Ethnic groups —Literary collections. 2. Minorities —Literary collections.
3. Cultural pluralism —United States. 4. United States —Ethnic relations. 5. United States —Race relations. 6. Minorities —United States. I. Title.

PS508.M54 C43 2012
810.8/0920693 —dc22
2011944309

COVER IMAGE AND INTERIOR IMAGE CREDITS

Tang Yong Lan, c. 1969, courtesy of Li Miao Lovett.
Samuel A. Autman, photo by Chris Walsh © 1999, courtesy of the author.
Buddhist monks, Thailand © by Katrina Grigg-Saito.
Woman weaving and her work, San Antonio Aguas Calientes, Antigua, Guatemala © 2010 by Gretchen Brown Wright.
On a road near Semuc Champey, Guatemala © 2011 by Gretchen Brown Wright.
Mision de San Francisco de Borja, Baja California Norte, Mexico © 2006 by Simmons B. Buntin.
Mision de Nuestra Senora de Loreto Concho, Loreto, Baja California Sur, Mexico © 2007 by Simmons B. Buntin.
Kelly and Nebras, photo by Kosuko Robinson © 2003, courtesy of Kelly Hayes-Raitt.
Sarah J. Stoner, *Kite Flying on Terra Firma, Calpé, Spain, 1980*, courtesy of the author.
Mixed Blood, 22" x 28", oil and pastel © 2004 by Christine Stark.

Continued on page 200

For Eileen Malone—without her, this book would not be in existence—and for my parents, cultural pioneers who found love in the pre–civil rights era.

CONTENTS

THE OTHER

THE CULTURE OF SELF AND SPIRIT

QUESTIONS FOR DISCUSSION

FOREWORD

I thought it was fitting that on the day I received the contract from Wyatt-MacKenzie to publish *The Chalk Circle: Intercultural Prizewinning Essays*—October 16, 2011—the Martin Luther King, Jr. National Memorial was dedicated in Washington, D.C. The ceremony was presided over by our first African American president (more serendipitous timing), but, in the background, a small controversy stirred: the memorial sculptor, Lei Yixin, is from China, and viewers felt that King's statue features were too Asian. Despite the fact that King's children approved the memorial, that the artist had great respect for Dr. King and had studied his face for years, the foundation had to defend its choice of artist.

This controversy propels me into a passionate discussion of why books such as *The Chalk Circle* are necessary, even in today's seemingly open-minded climate. Many dramatic advances in race relations have occurred since 1963 because of Dr. King, and the democratic invention of the *Inter*net has allowed cultural wrappings to become looser. Each day, however, incidents of prejudice and cultural misunderstandings still occur in all aspects of our social lives. One need only review recent news headlines to see how these misunderstandings can affect our business dealings and personal and political relationships. In one month alone, December 2011, I collected the following news reports: the Dutch architectural firm MVRDV set off a storm of protest over its Cloud design for two linked towers in Seoul, South Korea, as many felt the proposed mock-up closely evoked the 9/11 U.S. tragedy; a small Kentucky church banned interracial couples from membership in order to "promote greater unity," despite the fact that black-white marriages have more than tripled since 1980; in Cincinnati, Ohio, a white landlord posted a vintage 1931 Alabama sign on her rental home's gate stating: "Public Swimming Pool, Whites Only," in order to keep a black resident's teenage daughter out of the pool because of her use of certain hair products.

And in January 2012, Governor Jan Brewer was photographed pointing a finger in President Obama's face, setting off a firestorm of protest from African Americans: The gesture is considered to be a highly aggressive move in their community.

What unites all or most of these disturbing missteps is that each guilty party had some inkling they were in the wrong, but didn't anticipate the full import of their actions. They didn't know enough about the community they were insulting, nor did they try to find a more sensitive solution to their projects or problems. As mentioned, interracial marriages are climbing (the U.S. Census Bureau predicts that multiracial Americans will be the majority by midcentury); thus, the need for individuals and countries to reach across cultural borders in order to better understand fellow countrypersons and international partners will increase—and our quality of life and even our economic stability will depend on successful cultural interactions.

When I came across the term *intercultural* in 2006, it was new to me. I jumped on it. The buzzword at the time was, and still is, *multicultural*. But I fell in love with the *inter*-twinings of this other term. *Multi*, to me, means many and separate; *inter* begs to be more inclusive. So I started the annual Intercultural Essay contest, hosted by the Soul-Making Keats Literary Awards. My idea was to give adults and youths a voice in social matters. If you search the Internet for examples of multiculturalism, invariably you come across links to children's literature. Perhaps this is because we can discuss ethnic and race issues on a very basic, nonthreatening picture book level, but once a voice grows and becomes more full and wise, more threatening, we tend to shut it down. We are told it is not polite or politically correct (PC) to discuss these matters in public. Nor do many writers dare to write about them, for fear of backlash or being pigeonholed into their ethnic category.

So I can't relay how excited I was when I received my first batch of contest essays. What would I find? What topics would dare to be discussed? I was not disappointed. Christine Stark's "*Giiwe*: go home" took me on a fascinating, highly personal journey to a borderland I knew nothing about, and her journey still resonates with me years later. I realized the moment I finished her essay that I needed to make the essays public. It wasn't enough to read them myself and give an award.

The contest resonated with the entrants as well. Upon receiving his prize, Samuel Autman wrote: "The other thing you gave me was the phrase 'intercultural.' I was amazed at this idea. Distinct from multicultural. Even though I'm one of the darkest men you'll meet, I had always felt betwixt everything: race, gender, sexuality, spirituality. I grabbed [the phrase] quickly."

We hope you will grab on to *The Chalk Circle*'s essays just as hard, savor them, learn from them. It should be mentioned that because this book was not designed from scratch it does not represent every ethnicity. It's organic (covering ground from Germany to Japan to Guatemala), and, I think, pokes into more geographic and cultural corners than a text that is designed to reach certain PC parameters. Also, this book differs from other multicultural texts in that the voices are not all of color; represented in these pages are writers of Anglo-Saxon European descent as well, offering their points of view on controversial subjects. All voices need to be heard in order to find understanding and be truly intercultural. And these voices (appropriate for high school age or older) are vulnerable, strong, perceptive, intelligent, lyrical, journalistic, taking the reader down many different paths, both current and historic, both global and personal.

Format: Our goal is to introduce these skillful writers, both established and emerging, with more than the usual brief bio notes, hence the **fuller headnotes** meant to enhance the reading of each essay. These **twenty essays** are also grouped into **parts**, with subjects such as war and racism and food, headed by famous quotes; the parts are meant to give further weight to each essay when juxtaposed with its companion(s). (Note that while these contest essays all won a prize or honorable mention, we don't reveal their placings—all carry equal weight.) And for those who adopt this book in their book clubs or classrooms, we have included **Intercultural Considerations and Connections** to spark what we hope will be sensitive, thoughtful debates on topics readers may never before have encountered or been able to safely discuss in public. Included in the questions are **NET assignments** designed to get readers actively involved in the discussions, using contemporary technology. The book finishes with an invitation to explore the **part quotations**, one of which was chosen to title the book.

In 1845, Jane Carlyle wrote to her husband, essayist Thomas Carlyle, "Instead of boiling up individuals into the species—I would draw a chalk circle round every individuality and preach to it to keep within that, and preserve and cultivate its identity at the expense of ever so much lost giltlacker of other people's isms." Jane was ahead of her time.

We in this collection also believe in preserving and cultivating identity within a chalk circle, a medium that is common and permeable and allows for some migration across the individual boundaries.

INTRODUCTION

I

When I give readings of my work or speak on the issues of race or diversity or even when I first meet strangers at a social gathering, I find myself providing people with a simplified gloss on who I am. This starts with "My grandparents came here to America from Japan around 1905. I'm third generation." Sometimes I add that I'm a *Sansei*, the Japanese American term for third generation, and that my parents and their families were interned during World War II along with 120,000 other Japanese Americans. If people still ask me that inevitable question, "Where are you from?" I tell them, "I grew up in Chicago, in Skokie, a Jewish suburb."

Such a short summary, however, always feels truncated to me. I've written two memoirs, numerous essays, and three books of poetry, all of which explore my identity as a third generation Japanese American and the history of my community. And yet, even after all these writings, I feel I've only begun to scratch the surface of the questions I've been exploring.

For instance, as with many Americans, I grew up thinking of race mostly in terms of a dialog between whites and blacks. At the same time, if I thought about myself as a Japanese American, it was mainly in relationship with and comparison to the white majority. It was only in my thirties that I began to perceive that the questions about race and identity I was facing were more complex. In the space granted here I can't possibly enumerate the many experiences that have complicated my perspective on race, ethnicity, and identity, but here are a few brief examples.

In the early 1990s, I started the Asian American Renaissance, an arts organization in Minneapolis, and I soon came to realize that the organization had to take into account the specific concerns of a number of ethnic communities other than my own—Hmong, Vietnamese, Chinese, Cambodian, Lao, Thai, Indian, Korean, Filipino. In order to carry out this accounting, I had to make connections with people in those communities; I had to learn a lot more about their various cultures and histories.

A few years later, as a faculty member at VONA, a writers' conference for writers of color, I became friends with an array of celebrated writers from different backgrounds—Junot Díaz (Dominican), Elmaz Abinader (Lebanese), Chris Abani (Nigerian), Willie Perdomo (Puerto Rican), Cristina García (Cuban), Suheir Hammad (Palestinian), Staceyann Chin (Jamaican/black/Chinese), Lorna Dee Cervantes (Chicana), Quincy Troupe and ZZ Packer (African American). Many of these colleagues came from countries or ethnic heritages I knew little about, and I realized that if I was going to befriend them and understand their writing, I had a lot of work to do.

My life as a father has also changed my perspective on these issues. My children are half Japanese American, three-eighths WASP, and one-eighth Jewish, and this mixture is simply a reflection of the diversity of their world. Though the place where they've grown up, Minneapolis, is still thought of as predominantly white, students of color now make up over 60 percent of the student population. My children's elementary school contained students with thirty first languages; some of their friends came from backgrounds—Tibetan, Bosnian, Somalian, Ethiopian, Tunisian—that never even entered my consciousness when I was a child. Currently my youngest son is going out with a girl whose ethnicity is a quarter German, a quarter Thai, and half Puerto Rican; my other son and my daughter are both going out with Ethiopian Americans.

A couple of years ago, when my middle son, Nikko, was with a Somali Muslim American, my youngest son asked me, "Have you noticed that Nikko has stopped eating pork?" Though I grew up in a suburb where the Jewish American girls were not allowed to date me, the particular questions Nikko was facing were still a surprise to me. I hadn't expected that I would have to discuss with my son the possibility of his converting to Islam or the opposition of his girlfriend's Somali parents to their interethnic/interreligious/interracial relationship.

Eventually I wrote a poem about my son's relationship with this girl. In the poem I also allude to an interracial relationship my aunt had in high school with a white boy, just before her family was interned in World War II. It's a poem about the present, a poem about history, and like the essays in *The Chalk Circle*, it's a poem about how America is and always has been centered on the intercultural:

My Son at Ninth Grade

Overnight grown so towering, head wooly
with long curls, he'll stare me down eye
to eye. A black wisp over his lip he

won't shave. Hip-hop on iPod, beats
on Garage Band, poems on his Mac
book. And nights beneath the sheets

whispering on his cell to Yasmine,
a twenty-first century down low romance
her father and brothers would shut down

like a house of plague . . . if they discovered.
I pass his door and his voice lowers.
What does she see in him and he in her?

Only it's not sight, there in the dark,
but the words shuttling between them,
old as Romeo and Juliet, Sharks

and Jets, Buddha and Mohammed
and the mad crazy years we live in
where this young love fights to flourish.

(Two weeks later her brother shouts
the alarm to her father and mother. Now
there's a line that cannot be crossed,

and still I hear my son behind his door
weeping and whispering in the dark,
voices on the line, their secrets abhorred.)

Once a white boy fell in love with my aunt.
She left for the camps, never saw him again.
Ojii-san disapproved. Still from Japan.

Five young Somali men shot or knifed
last year in our precinct. Others vanished
to Mogadishu, war lords, civil strife.

The FBI, the police, what do they know?
Fathers, mothers, where's your daughter, your son?
Children, all this started so long ago.

Tonight as I make our bed, my son sneaks
in, leaps my back with his heavy new body;
and with war yelps wrestles me to the sheets.

Of course I don't let him beat me. Grunting
back, I toss him off like the years, grapple
his torso down, pinion each young wing,

though even as he cries out *I give, I give,*
assenting to the father, I cannot grip
him tight enough, I cannot let go.

II

The Chalk Circle: Intercultural Prizewinning Essays is a particularly timely and necessary anthology. To engage the America my children are growing up in, to explore our diversity and our globally connected world, these essays are a great place to start. In this stellar collection, there are thought-provoking meditations on family history that deal with difficult questions about fate, guilt, and personal responsibility—Li Miao Lovett on familial ties to China's landowning class, Shanti Elke Bannwart on being the daughter of a Nazi, Christine Stark on being both white and of American Indian ancestry. There are essays that skillfully examine the questions of race, such as Samuel Autman's subtle and ironic account of being a black man in Utah or the bravely honest examinations of white identity by Kelly Hayes-Raitt, Mary Elizabeth Parker, and

Lyzette Wanzer. Tilia Klebenov Jacobs recounts the ironic start of her parents' interreligious marriage while Emma Sartwell explores her dual religious heritage. Many of the writers explore intercultural experiences through travel, or highlight encounters with the foods and spiritual teachings of other cultures—Sarah J. Stoner, Katrina Grigg-Saito, Kamela Jordan, M. Garett Bauman, Jeff Fearnside, Bonnie J. Morris, Betty Jo Goddard, Gretchen Brown Wright, Simmons B. Buntin. The intersection between sexual preference and culture anchors Toshi Washizu's moving and delicate piece.

Throughout the book the writers find themselves exploring questions about identity:

> My thoughts heaved. I did not belong. I did belong. Maybe I could get help, real help, not Band-Aid therapy. I could not get help. I was "unhelpable." I was Indian. I was not Indian. (Christine Stark)

> I check the Caucasian box on forms; I feel guilt at the thought of slavery or Whites Only bathrooms; I never consciously feel that my race is a detriment, a consideration, or much of anything at all. (Emma Sartwell)

> Many times I wondered, Is this person staring because I am six-foot-four, black, or both? These are the unseen mental jumping jacks many people of color navigate when they live in cities and small towns where the citizens don't often have faces like their own. (Samuel Autman)

> My father was a Nazi, decorated by Hitler with the Iron Cross of Merit. (Shanti Elke Bannwart)

> Since I'm a mix of Japanese and white with whispers of black and Cherokee, nobody ever knows where I'm from, but they know I'm not from *here*, and *here* is always where I am. (Katrina Grigg-Saito)

These quotations illustrate a basic point: Identity cannot be thought of without difference, that is, without considering what I am not. Thus identity is question concerning one's position in the world: I am like and I am not like. I belong and I do not belong. And yet, at the same time, we are all human, we are all connected, despite our differences. The tensions within such questions are multiple. For the writers here, these questions are sometimes vexing or troublesome; at other times—especially in the section on food—the questions are explored with delight, even celebration.

Not far into my reading of *The Chalk Circle*, I began to think of a boy whose mother was a white American, mostly of English ethnic heritage, from Kansas, and whose father was of the Luo ethnic group from Kenya. The two met in Hawaii, as students, and soon after the son was born, they were divorced. The mother then married a Javanese man and moved to Jakarta, Indonesia, where the boy went to school with other Muslim Indonesian children (thus making him what Sarah Stoner calls in her essay a Third Culture Kid, an American raised abroad). At ten the boy returned to Hawaii where he went to the Punahou School where the students were white, Asian American (Japanese, Chinese, Korean, Filipino), Hawaiian, and Pacific Islander. Later in adolescence the boy began seeking contacts with other African Americans, both his age and older, in order to understand what his identity might be as a black man in America.

This boy grew up with a range of experiences with other peoples and cultures that neither of his parents could have foreseen. Nor of course did they foresee that he would eventually grow up to become the 44th President of the United States.

Barack Obama has been designated our first black President, and many see him as akin to other American blacks, but in various ways, such a designation ignores both sides of his parental heritage. Other misperceptions abound. Though Obama has declared himself a Christian, he has been called a Muslim. Though he is an American citizen, a portion of the population believes he was not born here, and he has been called a Mau Mau Kenyan anti-colonialist. What is clear is that many people, even some of his supporters, cannot somehow come to terms with the complexities of his background and experiences. They wish to simplify his identity, his past, and his parentage.

For me the essays in *The Chalk Circle* brought to mind Obama's wonderful autobiography, *Dreams from My Father: A Story of Race and Inheritance*. They share with that memoir an openness to complex questions of identity, whether those questions involve ethnicity, race, religion, culture, politics, or history. The writers in this collection make abundantly clear that our 44th President's complex background is not an aberration or an isolated instance, but simply an emblem of who we are and what we have become.

III

Each of the pieces in *The Chalk Circle* is a snapshot of America today, in 2012—a country of unprecedented ethnic and racial diversity. In a few decades this country will no longer be characterized by a white majority, and these essays can be read as attempts to grapple with this coming shift and to redefine what it means to be an American in light of this inevitable change.

At the same time, *The Chalk Circle* is about what it means to be a citizen of the world. As Pulitzer Prize–winning author Thomas L. Friedman has reminded us, because of recent advances in technology and commerce, the countries and peoples of our globe have become increasingly and complexly interconnected. No place or people can be viewed simply as separate and isolated entities. The essays included here come out of this sense of the world.

There's a quotation from American novelist and essayist James Baldwin that I often cite as emblematic of our times. It provides a useful gloss to this collection:

> The question of identity is a question involving the most profound panic—a terror as primary as the nightmare of the mortal fall. . . . An identity is questioned only when it is menaced, as when the mighty begin to fall, or when the wretched begin to rise, or when the stranger enters the gates, never, thereafter, to be a stranger: the stranger's presence making *you* the stranger, less to the stranger than to yourself. Identity would seem to be the garment with which

one covers the nakedness of the self; in which case, it is best that the garment be loose, a little like the robes of the desert, through which robes one's nakedness can always be felt, and sometimes, discerned. This trust in one's nakedness is all that gives one the power to change one's robes.

— from *The Devil Finds Work*

As evidenced by the recent political protests and events in the Middle East, we live in a world today where the wretched are rising up and taking on new identities. At the same time, we live in a world and an America where stranger is encountering stranger with increasing frequency. Through such meetings both strangers must reconsider and reconfigure who they think they are and who they think the stranger is. Bearing witness to this process, the intercultural essays of *The Chalk Circle* will help readers, as Baldwin advises, to wear their robes loosely, to be prepared for changing them again and again.

— David Mura
Stonecoast MFA Program, University of Southern Maine

THE CHALK CIRCLE: IDENTITY, HOME, AND BORDERLANDS

> *"Instead of boiling up individuals into the species, I would draw a chalk circle round every individuality, and preach to it to keep within that, and preserve and cultivate its identity."*

> — Jane Welsh Carlyle (1801–1866) to Thomas Carlyle, August 5, 1845

Li Miao Lovett grew up in San Francisco's Chinatown, an enclave of tradition, language, and superstition. She emigrated from Taiwan, where her father's family had settled in 1949 as refugees from mainland China. Lovett has an MA in psychology and a BA from Stanford University, where she began exploring her cultural roots through drama, dance, and social activism. She has been a frequent contributor to the *San Francisco Chronicle* and Perspectives on KQED, a leading NPR radio station. Her literary and environmental writing have appeared in *Narrative Magazine, Earth Island Journal, China Rights Forum,* and *Stanford Magazine*. She has organized events for Words Without Borders, featuring Alice Walker and other writers reading from translated literature. In both fiction and nonfiction, Lovett's work has won awards or finalist standing from *Glimmer Train, Writer's Digest,* the Stanford Fiction Contest, A Room of Her Own Foundation's Orlando Prize, and the James Jones First Novel Fellowship. Her debut novel, *In the Lap of the Gods* (2010), portrays the lives of those uprooted by China's Three Gorges dam. "A compelling, sometimes damning portrait" of the Three Gorges project (Barnes & Noble review), the novel would likely be banned in China.

If Grandmother Had Married a Peasant

Li Miao Lovett

In the face of my father's sister, I see my own. It's a broad face with high cheekbones, copper-toned skin, and a nose shaped like a garlic bulb. Pulling my coarse, black hair into a bun, I am Mao's poster child, the idealized peasant.

I always thought that I came from a long line of peasants, on both sides of my family. Only recently did I learn that my mother's mother had lived an aristocrat's life until the death of the last Chinese dynasty, and the births of seven children that gradually transformed her into a poor but proud housewife.

My father's family also endured the legacy of riches to rags. His father was a landowner in Shandong, in northeastern China, where winters were harsh and the men were big-boned and hot-tempered. In the wake of World War II, the Communists stormed through their village. My grandfather was tortured until the family coffers

1

were drained, and my grandmother, a gentle and unassuming woman, even considered poisoning him to relieve his suffering. In 1949, my father and his family fled from the Communists on a three-day journey by foot, and then on a military boat with the defeated Nationalists to Taiwan. Twenty years later, my father made a second escape, a welcomed journey to America that unshackled him from the legacies of family and war.

Growing up in the alleyways of San Francisco's Chinatown, I never imagined a different life—the life I could have led in the old country. My family's memories of China were tucked away in secret compartments, and the tales of my father's ordeal as a refugee came in hushed asides through my mother. I understood, through these whisperings, through my parents' unspoken expectations, that my life was better because of the choices they had made. Mother told me there were starving children in China less fortunate than I, but even as we rose into the ranks of the middle class, I did not think of myself as the more privileged one. In this country, there was always more that one could desire, dream of, and obtain.

Thirty years later, the questions surrounding fortune and fate have taken a new turn. In a teacher's magazine, I came across a photo of young women working in a Chinese factory, surrounded by a monstrous pile of doll heads ready to be screwed onto pink, plastic bodies. In these factories, the women worked up to 18 hours a day, in grinding 100-degree heat, surrounded by the smell of plastic and chemicals. Most of the workers came from the countryside, and they endured low wages and employer abuse so that they could earn a little money to send back home. I stared at the image of one of the girls. She had a broad face with a bulbous nose and rosy cheeks; it was a peasant's face, not so different from mine. I began to ask the *what if?* questions.

What if my grandmother, my father's mother, had married a peasant, instead of a landowner who was persecuted for his wealth and forced to flee his homeland more than half a century ago?

If grandmother had married a peasant man, they may have greeted the new Communist regime with hope. When the blood of revolution had dried from the fields, the land would be theirs to till. The masses would be organized into collectives, ten and twenty thousand to a commune. This would be the triumph of Communism, where each man, woman, and child would no longer suffer from hunger or privation, as long as she or he gave himself to the state.

I imagine the features of the man who would be my father. Perhaps this man would have possessed my grandmother's gaunt cheeks, and her quiet forbearance in the face of life's unjust blows. As a toddler, my imagined father would be strapped close to his mother's bosom, lulled by the swaying of her body toward stoked fire and threshed wheat. When he was old enough to wield a plow, he would learn to strike the earth until his bare hands became leathered, tougher than the ragged fibers of his shoes. He would know no other classroom than the lessons of a harsh land, the prophecies of each planting season.

As he grew older, this father would know famine, the gnawing hunger of a generation that survived the Great Leap Forward. He would count the grains in his rice bowl, glad to be among the living while countless millions had died. He would wipe the soot off his father's face after a day and night of work in the village furnaces. He dared not question the patriotism of smelting pans for steel while their crops rotted in the field. He would trace the skeletons of Chinese characters in the dirt, not knowing the calligraphy had been simplified in the cultural cleansing of Mao Zedong's vision for a new China.

My real father has a university degree from Oklahoma State. Immigrating to America with a little seed money from a wealthy uncle, he took what jobs he could in those early years—busboy, dishwasher, and cook. When we moved to San Francisco, he became a computer technician, earning a salary that afforded private school for his only daughter in the 1970s and '80s.

My father placed a high value on education, a legacy of Confucian ethics that had structured the dynasties of China for four thousand years. He rarely speaks about the past, but when he remembers what the Communists did to his homeland, he speaks of "eating bitterness" in his understated way. When the tormentors placed his father on tables stacked to the ceiling and threatened to topple the landowning class, the old man no longer loomed large in my father's eyes. At last they had something in common, the fear of being punished. After several rounds of imprisonment and torture, my grandfather turned over all his property, which would be redistributed among landless peasants. Under Communist orders, the children were taken out of classrooms and put into the fields. As a six-year-old, my father learned harsh lessons about dignity. The peasants who had suffered under the scourge of feudalism were vindicated at last. He was the son of an evil landlord. His books were worthless, and his early education came from the blisters imposed by the stubborn soil of the Shandong countryside.

In 1997, I spent a month studying ancient Chinese teachings at a Taoist hermitage in Moscow, Idaho, where I tilled the land every day like a peasant—just as my father had been forced to do until the family's exodus. Beyond this six-acre plot, the endless furrows of green pastures rolled far into the horizon. I marveled at the smell of the earth under my fingernails, the firmness of summer squash, and the soft and yielding soil on my crouching legs. In the evenings, I practiced *qigong* with a martial arts master from mainland China, and with his American wife.

One day, while extracting the stubborn roots of a thistle embedded deep in the flower beds, I saw the irony of tilling the soil on this man's land. Until the 1980s, this *qigong* master had governed a commune of thirty thousand people in China. He was proud of the control he exerted as a middle manager in the Communist ranks. He spoke of the privileges enjoyed by this ruling class, fancy dinners with the politburo, the expensive habits of his teenage daughter. I wondered what the other thirty thousand ate for supper, how they lived. Knowing my own stint of peasant life was a voluntary one, I shuddered inside. And remembering the roots of my father's bitterness, I held my tongue.

The Communist government began sowing the seeds of a new market economy two decades ago. Now capitalism in China is no longer a scourge and a weed, but a blossoming fruit, even as the old Communist guard remains strong.

I continued staring at the portrait of the young woman surrounded by doll torsos, pink as erasers and decapitated. The woman's face seemed devoid of desire, but a quiet will came through in the firm lines of her jaw. My thoughts wandered again to an imagined life in China. If Grandmother had indeed married a peasant, would her son have tried to escape the peasant's life? Perhaps after surviving the terrible famines of a Great Leap that failed, my imagined father would decide to chance a life in the city. The first factories catering to the West would be springing up, and in the slums of Shanghai he would make a home for his new family. His wife would give birth to one child, a daughter. Alas, she is a girl, but she will work for her keep.

What would my life be like as this peasant father's daughter? Would I struggle with the same questions of livelihood and life purpose? Or would I find myself in the confines of a life scripted for me?

At the age of ten, I begin working at the local tanning factory. I am assigned to help the older workers, who tan the leather in giant rotating drums filled with putrid chemicals. Their fingers are ragged and blistered from handling the wet, limp hides for twelve, sometimes fourteen hours a day. My hands, too, are beginning to look like an old pair of men's boots. When I am twelve, I graduate to seamstress work at the shoe factory, laying the swatches of suede and woven fabric evenly beneath the relentless needles of my sewing machine. In this room there are dozens of girls my age. We rarely speak. The sound of the machines drowns out any words like the pounding of a hundred small jackhammers.

Sometimes, I stare out the dusty window at the jagged peaks of the distant mountains. The sky grows dark. I hear stories about Westerners climbing these great mountains, and wonder why anyone would venture into those fearsome clouds.

Growing up in America, I knew little about the wild places that existed beyond the concrete hills of San Francisco. Like other immigrant families, our idea of vacation wasn't camping out in primitive places; this was too close to the peasant's old way of life. Mountains were dark, looming objects my family drove by on the way to casino country, whose cities sparkled with the allure of instant jackpots and all-you-can-eat dinners. I didn't discover the splendor of starry desert skies and cragged mountaintops until I was an adult.

In the summer of 2001, I decided to go on an extended

backpacking trip on the southern part of the Appalachian Trail. I would walk from Springer Mountain, Georgia, along the border of North Carolina and Tennessee, into the highlands of Virginia. I needed sturdy gear for two months, a rugged backpack, a rain jacket to shield me from those summer storms, and a sturdy pair of boots.

Four days into the trip, my boots began to fray at the seams. I spent forty minutes that afternoon with a safety pin, driving it down into two layers of thick leather, then angling the needle back toward the surface with a blind thrust, careful to keep my fingers out of the way. My fingertips felt raw and spent, but I was pleased at my ingenuity. A week later, I had a new pair of boots waiting at the post office of a town near the trail. These boots were made in China, by a girl whose fingers had traveled many times over rubber soles that would journey a thousand miles.

I hiked up to ten hours a day, across the roller coaster of hills that at first left me breathless hour upon hour. Every night, I slept under the stars, or in simple three-walled shelters built for long-distance hikers. At dusk, mosquitoes whistled their hunting tunes, and after dark, lumbering black bears crashed through the woods with thunderous steps to follow the scent of a hiker's bag of treats. In the Great Smokies, summer thunderstorms would turn the trail into a flowing creek, and my sweat-stained clothes refused to dry that entire week.

But behind the hardship was freedom. I loved the smell of the soil, not because I was forced to tame and cultivate it, as my father did more than half a century ago, but because each step led me to the next unknown. My decision to quit a full-time faculty job with all its trappings and retirement benefits would be sealed that summer under a canopy of aspen and fir.

At one of the hiking hostels, someone had pointed out the irony of it all: "Top Ten Reasons for Doing the Appalachian Trail . . . #1. Quit your eight-hour-a-day, five-day-a-week job so that you can work twelve hours a day, seven days a week on the trail."

In the end, the agonizing choices and decisions of the privileged Westerner lose their meaning. As the only daughter of Chinese immigrants, I have gnashed my teeth over a confusing palette of life choices. Which path leads to the better life? All those books challenging us to follow our dreams imply that we will be happier if we only make the right choice. Or perhaps our mothers and grandmothers should have made the right choice. But none of us can truly know what life has in store. And so the question becomes—am I willing to lead my life, wherever it takes me?

My grandmother probably never wondered if she had made the right choice in marrying my grandfather. How could she have known that revolution would turn landowners into exiles, and peasants into their oppressors? And even if she did, she could never have foreseen the full weight of joys and sorrows in her life, and my father's, and mine. I've always thought that I was lucky to be incarnated as a Chinese American woman who could reap all the cultural pleasures and opportunities my native sisters could not. But if the soul's dignity is the true marker of a life well lived, then I can no longer say that I am the more privileged one.

In that picture, the young woman in the doll factory speaks to me. She holds her chin high, as if royal blood once ran through her veins. She speaks of a childhood running through endless fields, verdant in spring and bitterly cold in winter. And she tells me of those seeds she worked so hard to sow. The fruits they reap are no different than mine.

Sarah J. Stoner is an American-born writer who was raised in Uganda, Morocco, Belgium, and Thailand. Her subject matter most often touches on nature, mothering, and the experience of growing up outside of her home culture. Her work has appeared in numerous literary magazines and journals, such as *Marco Polo Quarterly, Get Born, Parent & Child*, and *The Journal for the Association for the Advancement of International Education*. She was a featured author for the City of Seattle Office of Arts and Cultural Affairs project—*TreeStory*—which launched a recent documentary of the same name by filmmaker Ward Serrill. Her family's roots run four generations deep in the Pacific Northwest where she now lives with her husband and two children—off-the-grid on a twenty-acre community land trust.

Fragments: Finding Center

Sarah J. Stoner

This year, I celebrate a life equinox.

I have lived in America exactly as many years as I have lived outside of America. At thirty-six, the perfect equilibrium of eighteen years on either side of the world simplifies the muddle of culture and identity and belonging that often throws me off balance.

The scale measured in years now tips toward America, my birth country. Soon, I will have lived in the United States longer than I lived overseas. My international identity disappears deeper below the surface of my freckled white skin. I fear a strange sort of American-induced amnesia as my expatriate experiences settle like stones, untended, on the bottom of a river.

I never knew that I was a Third Culture Kid, or TCK, until my early thirties. More precisely, it was then that I learned my experience of growing up in the international school system had a name. Because I grew up outside of my home country (my first culture), in a country that was not my own (a second culture), I lived in a third culture created from belonging to neither, and being from both—sort of.

Yes, I'm a Third Culture Kid.

I was relieved to finally have a shortened version of, "Well, I am American but I never lived in America until college. I went to high school in Thailand and before that I lived in Belgium and then Morocco before that. Yes, I was born in the U.S. but we left for Uganda when I was seventeen days old."

My childhood experience had a name. Growing up in an international school community was a classifiable collective experience described in a handful of books with long-term studies to boot. The discovery threw a grounding tether from my present life backward. And helped me tap into the angst I carry with me as I float through my life in America, mostly tightlipped about my childhood.

My parents lived and worked as international school teachers and administrators for more than forty years, starting in the late 1960s. I grew up in international schools of Kampala, Rabat, Antwerp, and Bangkok through the 1970s and 1980s. At the time, little research or literature was focused on the TCK student. With increased awareness in the last decade of this unique collective identity, I understand that we TCKs each have a unique story to tell.

My story is similar in that it is different from every other TCK's. It reflects the fact that I lived the first half of my life playing and learning outside of my birth country. But at eighteen, I swung my life "home" to the United States. Home? A TCK-authored book title—*According To My Passport, I'm Going Home*—offers a pithy reflection of my relationship to "home."

Fall 1988. I arrive in the Pacific Northwest with a vague memory of moss and two suitcases. My mother had flown with me for the transition from Bangkok, my home for the last five years, to college in the States. I'd just graduated high school and spent summer in Bangkok, partying up, numbing out, not ready.

We touch down. A few days in Seattle with my uncle, a visit to the Puyallup Fair—large turkeys, large bits of sugar-coated fried dough, and large white people—for a quick cultural emersion. Next: north to a lush college town I'd never visited. Western Washington University enrollment begins.

My mother, my brother, and I barrel north from Seattle up Interstate 5. We drive past the car lots of Everett, past the strip malls of Burlington, into the calm green corridor that cuts through Bellingham, Washington.

I look out the window. Late afternoon light falls on new terrain—evergreen trees, smooth highway, zipping cars, and green green green. No turning back. I swallow the rising tightness in my throat.

My brain steps in, offers a mantra to rationalize away the fear: I chose this, this college whose campus I've never visited. I chose this, going to college in the United States rather than studying in Europe.

What I had chosen, in essence, was the ability to answer one specific question with more solidity: "Where are you from?"

Overseas, the question implied nationality. I'd answer, "I'm American." Summer holidays, often spent traveling in the States, I'd answer based on the home I was away from. "I live in Bangkok."

My soul felt ready to root, to burrow into my birth country's soil. Roots and wings, root and wings. I had the wings. Eighteen years strong of flying every five years from country to country. With sinewy ease, I land in a new culture, join a new flock, and reemerge. New rules, new language, new me.

Now, where was I from again?

I was born in Los Angeles, California. But this is not where I am from.

My mother and father were born in Vancouver, Washington. But this is not where I am from. This is where they are from. They lived their childhoods in their respective family homes. My mother's parents—teachers at the local school. My father's parents—homemaker and shoe repairman.

Somehow, from this blue-collar town of mill workers and dairy farmers and chain restaurants, sprang my mother, ever curious and adventuresome. As a little girl on the bus, she would gradually move forward toward a different accent until she sat in the seat just behind the foreign-sounding conversation, her entire body rigid, listening, intrigued.

My mother and father married three years after high school. She somehow convinced my father to join the newly formed Peace Corps and haul off to West Africa. He grew up so apple pie that he'd never even eaten an avocado, but he signed on for the adventure. They taught English for two years in a remote Liberian village.

My father tasted his first avocado. I think he liked it.

Forty years later, they still live overseas.

They must have hit their life equinox sometime in the late 1980s, around when I was eighteen.

It is September. I am eighteen, in the backseat of a midsize rental car, standard American sedan, zooming toward my new life. The narrow chute of I-5 is my birth canal. The lump in my throat keeps the tears at bay. I have never been to Bellingham, Washington. I have never lived in America.

My mother and brother will drop me off at my dorm on campus, meet my new dormmate, then drive back to Seattle. My mother has a flight to catch across the Pacific Ocean, back to Bangkok, to start the new teaching year at my old school.

Tomorrow, I will wake up alone on the continent.

My stomach aches, a tight balloon of emptiness.

It had been an empty summer, that first summer after high school. The chasm of loss already started. My community fell away, one after the other plunging like skydivers out of a plane, disappearing too fast into new lives. My best friend, Franc: already in Holland, starting school. My high school boyfriend, Andreas: back to his home town in Bavaria. Even my father: gone.

He left for his new job in Frankfurt, my parents' divorce conveniently scheduled for the end of my senior year, delayed so we could all disband at once. It had been a horrible year at home.

In the backseat, my body sits still in the car moving up I-5 at 60 miles an hour. I am somewhere else, too scared to inhabit my body. I might throw up if I feel all of my fear.

Maybe this is what it's like to be adopted, on the way to meet your birth parents for the first time. You are strangers—though intimately *of* them. As much as your adoptive parents may love you, and you love them, a deep secret part of you knows that you do not wholly belong.

My husband is adopted and I wonder—is this a part of our shared experience? Growing up among worlds, somehow, touches the same core wound. Who am I? Where do I belong? Where is home?

But the identity of being adopted is handled with care. People know and assume the inherent trauma and angst of growing up removed from the flesh and safety of your birth mother.

The identity of growing up removed from your home country invites applause, awe, and many, many assumptions—thoughts of worldliness, culture, adventure. My upbringing is romanticized, exoticized, revered. No one wants to hear about the shadow side, about an inexplicable angst of growing up removed from the solid identity of your birth country.

By Halloween of my first year in America, I stopped talking about where I was from.

Third Culture Kids like me know that fitting in is key to survival in a culture. My training started young, barely out of the womb in Africa. Blending in as a freshman at a state university in a town of 120,000 meant camouflaging my self.

If my identity emerged, I could count on one of two reactions. Both of them created distance between me and the other: the opposite of fitting in, of belonging.

So—fitting in—as an American in America who's never lived in America:

Take One. Fitting In. The scene: A group of college freshmen, young women and men, mill around a dented metal keg, red plastic cups in common, bonding us instant beer buddies.

The conversation is about nothing, and everything. The familiar tribes of our respective high schools lay behind us, disbanded. We are all in new territory, jockeying for our place, sniffing for others of our tribe.

My light brown hair, pale blue eyes, and fair skin betray me. Apparently I look like someone who went to everyone's high school.

A keg-circle girl in a purple sweater turns to me. "Hey, you look familiar. I think you went to my high school," she says.

"Nooooooo, I don't think so," I say, tilting my head to the side. Avoiding offering more information.

"Oh, you didn't go to Issaquah High? Gosh, I could have sworn you did," she says, followed by the polite white follow-up question: "Where did you go?"

"Um, well, I went to high school in Bangkok, Thailand," I say.

Poof, the words make me disappear. I suddenly no longer exist in her eyes. Friendly explorative tone: gone. Eye contact: gone. Body language: turned away from me. I think she utters, "Oh," before she turns away to someone wearing a baseball cap that reads BLANCHETT.

I am too much effort to uncover, an historical excavation

when all she wants is small-talk connection. In the search for common ground, clearly, I am not one of her tribe. I am a strange Other and she moves on. Fast.

Take 2: Fitting In. The scene: "Wow! You went to high school in Thailand? Omigosh, I've always wanted to go to Asia. What's it like? You must be *so* cool," he says.

This guy has known me for all of three seconds, and all of a sudden I'm the hottest thing since fried rice. In his eyes, I am different, and therefore, better.

I stare into my plastic keg cup as he tells me how much more I know than anyone else in the room, how much more I have already experienced in my life. I humor him with a few stories about partying in Patpong, Bangkok's red light district.

We have nothing in common. He doesn't know Thailand, he doesn't know me. He wants my stories and his impression of me.

I stare at the pattern of my sluggish beer foam as if I were staring at tea leaf fortunes in a mug. I wish for an ethnic look, or a foreign accent, an easy category of difference that doesn't confuse or mislead. I look and sound American. My lack of physical identifier as "different" makes the way I eat my fries in the mess hall—with my fork and knife, like any regular European teen—appear nonsensical and freakish. If I had Asian features, or spoke with a British accent, my behavior (behaviour!) would be excused. But get a load of that plain Jane eating her fries with a fork. What's her deal?

Note to self: Eat fries with fingers when in America.

By omission of my background, and by eating fries like my peers, I could pretty much pretend I belonged.

Ah, but there are no CliffsNotes for that one impenetrable road block to my complete social inclusion: television.

Television characters, theme songs, and sitcom episodes pepper American relationships. From *Schoolhouse Rock* ("Conjunction junction, what's your function?") to *The Brady Bunch* to *Saturday Night Live*, born-and-bred Americans unconsciously incorporate cultural cues from their lives growing up with television shows. Like the weather, television talk exists as an elemental conversation piece that most red-blooded Americans can participate in. Not me.

I am left out when my peers bond about which *Gilligan's*

Island episode mirrors the moment we just experienced. I seem aloof, rude, or clueless when I don't laugh at the group joke about our dinner hosts acting like Mike and Carol. Who is Mike Brady and why are we talking about him? I think blankly.

A pronounced British accent or status as an exchange student would work wonders for me in this moment. But my bland and unremarkable exterior offers no such grace. I appear deceptively American. I should know what's so damned funny about *The Brady Bunch* reference.

I have lived in the United States long enough now to feel the flow of the year through the rhythm of television. Deprive me of sensory input of nature: natural light, a view of deciduous trees, the sky—and I won't know what time of the year it is. But give access to American TV, and like a native who navigates the shadows and light of the sun, I can tell you: Those two-hour finales signal the coming of summer and reruns, the dormant season for our flickering friend. New shows signal fall and the start of a new school year.

Parts of me exist only in a particular country at a particular moment in time. Truth is, I haven't found a way to connect the pieces.

My babyhood patters along the cool floors of my first home in Uganda. My childhood clomps under Morocco's bright sun, dressed in my favorite green clogs. Those pre-teen years, plumped up from tasty Flemish candy, wander the halls of a small school in Belgium. The ghosts of my teenage years, too much freedom and quiet hurts, throb through Bangkok's bars and wild streets.

You can never step in the same river twice, yes. But sediment from my journey bumps unseen against my insides, sinks and rises depending on the current.

Slowly, I leave behind the little girl who spoke French, English, and Arabic all in one breath. Silted memories—steeped in the scents of Africa, Europe, Asia—drop at a slow corner on the bend. The stones of my childhood sit quietly at the bottom. For now, they have no place in the flow.

I recognize that who I am depends on the slant of light that shines on me; for now—that sun is American.

Eighteen years after coming "home," I may not regularly watch television. I still miss out on many cultural references—

this time by choice. Today, my inability to participate in media-culture conversations is an unquestioned preference rather than a long story I have to tell.

There's power in not having to explain myself. It dulls that sharp edge of angst, of feeling like an Other.

I came to the United States to reconcile my Otherness, and I did.

Planted solidly in my American life, I have ease and peace in being able to now say, comfortably, that I am American. I no longer experience the strangeness of claiming to be from a land in which I've never lived.

After having lived eighteen years on U.S. soil, I've found my way, made my place—my friends, my community. Moss runs through my veins, alongside the joy of fresh rains and four seasons and belonging. The green that surrounds me is home.

Base camp, at least.

Christine Stark is an award-winning writer and visual artist of European and American Indian ancestry whose work has been published in numerous periodicals and anthologies, including *The Florida Review; Feminist Studies; Poetry Motel; Hawk & Handsaw; To Plead Our Own Cause: Narratives of Modern Slavery;* and *Primavera.* She is coeditor (with Rebecca Whisnant) of *Not for Sale,* an international anthology on sexual violence. Stark, a Pushcart Prize nominee, won a 2010 Loft Mentorship in creative nonfiction. In 2011 her poem "Momma's Song" was released as a CD in collaboration with musician Fred Ho, and her debut novel, *Nickels,* was published by Modern History Press and is a Lambda Literary Award finalist as of this printing. Stark has an MFA in Creative Writing from Minnesota State University at Mankato, and currently she teaches writing at Metropolitan State University and lives with her partner in Minneapolis.

Giiwe: go home

Christine Stark

I lost twenty-nine drawings and paintings when someone set fire to the turn-of-the-century two-story brick building on Cedar and 16th in south Minneapolis on January 17, 2004. Whoever did it started the fire on the second floor and burned it down into the gallery. Three weeks after the fire my mother died from complications after fourteen months of chemotherapy. She was one treatment away from remission. I thought I had finally found my way home after winding across the country for years (Minnesota to Wisconsin to Minnesota to Oregon to Florida to Minnesota), but the fire and the death of my mother inched me further up the spine of Minnesota, until I landed a few hours from the Canadian border in the northwestern corner, perched on the lip of North Dakota, five minutes off the White Earth reservation.

I've come home, or so I've been told. The *manidoog* want me here, in this whitewashed expanse of drifting blowing snow and farm land clear cut by the Norwegian, German, and Swedish immigrants and their mixed-blood offspring 125 years ago. Part white, part Anishinaabe, they and the full-blood Europeans reversed the millennial growth of the forest in a few decades. The mixed bloods removed the home of their Indian ancestors so that the Europeans would have one. It was a true borderland life, constantly negotiating cultures from all over the world that landed on that particular spot of earth at that particular time in history to establish something called America. To create—out of anger, hatred, expediency, greed, and sometimes love—people who carry two opposing cultures in their skin. People like me.

After years of arguing with myself and various friends over whether I had any right to be part of Indian communities (I said I did not, my friends said I did), I finally made the leap and organized an art show discussion series aptly titled *Amerika: Land of Rape and Genocide*. It consisted mostly of my work, over forty drawings and paintings, along with the healing masks of Samantha Emery; American Indian dolls created by my friend Sherri; and the work of women from Breaking Free, an Afro-centric organization that helps women recover from sexual and physical violence. At the time, I was facilitating an art group at Breaking Free, and the women had made splendid masks of their faces out of plaster and bright paint to evoke the pain, trauma, and hope of their lives. Working with the Minnesota Indian Women's Sexual Assault Coalition, I'd scheduled a series of talks to address violence against American Indian and African American women. I wanted to get to the heart of it: genocide and slavery.

The morning after the first meeting—a panel that addressed the history of American Indian and African American women's sexual violence, healing, and activism—our arsonist flicked his Bic and turned our art and a one-hundred-year-old building into smoke and ice-encrusted rubble. While the building burned, I stood in a crowd across the street, wincing as the firefighters sprayed arcs of water into the building, which then sheeted down the interior walls and drenched the art that had escaped the flames. A woman standing on the sidewalk next to me said, *There's always trouble on this corner,* and nodded toward the cemetery next to the building. *Car accidents. Shootings. Fights. Drugs.* Others nodded knowingly.

The southwest section of the gallery was less damaged and, despite being told not to by the fire chief, I surreptitiously slid my way through the slush-covered street, inching closer and closer to the section where my newest pieces clung to the brick walls, knocked sideways by the force of the water and reverberations of the falling brick above. Some of them looked perfectly fine despite the carnage around them, their faces gleaming through the gray and icy day, while others looked soggy, yet alive.

I talked up two firemen standing next to me, their arms folded across their chests and their oversized tan canvas suits, as they waited for orders. Much to my surprise they waded across the blocked-off street through the front door, into the less damaged part of the gallery, and grabbed twelve of my newest pieces—the ones that dealt with my intense and often painful feelings of having European, Anishinaabe, and Cherokee ancestry. They, too, had orders from the fire chief that no one was to enter the building for any reason. When they returned with my art, I scribbled my home phone number on a scrap of paper in case they caught hell for entering the building and needed me to come to their defense. I took one last look at the smoldering inferno and then loaded my soggy art into the cab of my black Ford Ranger and headed home to north Minneapolis.

The fire and the death of my mother did not drive me out of Minneapolis, but they did set my final move toward home in motion. Since I'd left my parents' place at nineteen, I'd moved one to two times every year for nine years inside the city limits of Madison, Wisconsin. I eventually moved back to the Twin Cities, then decided that I needed to leave home in order to find home, so I headed to the west coast with my partner.

When I lived in Portland, Oregon, I felt lost, alien to the temperate climate, gray drizzle, distant mountains, and the heavy mustiness that pervaded everything, especially the stacks at Powell's Bookstore where I worked. I did not like being two to three hours behind the rest of the country. I did not like the people. They struck me as rude, exclusive, and too hip for their own—or anyone else's—good. Some difficulties at my partner's workplace were all we needed to set off across the country, heading south, our puppy sick with giardia in the passenger's seat of the U-Haul and me following in my red '92 Mazda hatchback with two foaming cats draped over the seats like fur stoles. We rumbled through Oregon and Idaho. In Utah, at a McDonald's parking lot, we scrambled to put our puppy and cats in their respective vehicles when two cowboys sauntered toward our assemblage. We figured they saw the rainbow sticker. I imagined a beating, our animals hurt. *Nice to see some family 'round here*, one of them said and tipped his hat. We set down the animals' cages and talked.

If I felt lost in Oregon, I was sunk in Florida. There it became apparent to me that I could not know myself if I was off the land I belonged to. I physically and spiritually yearned for Minnesota. I missed the woods, the lakes, the four seasons, the cold and snow, and the smell of freshwater lakes. I missed the foliage of Minnesota—high brush cranberries, sumac, towering pale purple lilac bushes, rhubarb, and white pines tall as four-story buildings. I did not like the fire ants, the sultry heat, the downpour that blasted Orlando for half an hour every afternoon at two, and the threat of alligators consuming my puppy in one gulp at virtually any watering hole. Bright blue and green peacocks scratched across rooftops and cabbagelike palm leaves waved beneath a cloudless sky. It was surreal. I was living in a foreign land. I would have moved back to Minnesota after one month, but we could not break our nine-month lease at the apartment complex. So I suffered the heat and the ants and the alligators, carrying my puppy up and down the outdoor black metal mesh staircase that he refused to stand on, terrified because he could see the ground beneath his paws.

I returned to Minnesota, to my mother's house in Bloomington, driving through an Iowa snowstorm with my dog and a few belongings. After a week-long search for an affordable apartment that accepted animals, I flew back to Orlando and drove our entire household over the Tennessee mountains and through the blue hills of Kentucky to our seventies chalet-style drug-dealer infested apartment in St. Paul. We were fortunate, though, to find a place at all. The housing market was tight—less than 1 percent vacancy because, according to friends of mine, the powers-that-be were interested in keeping out low-income folks, particularly black people from Illinois who supposedly move to Minnesota to take advantage of the welfare system.

I had been trying to find home since I was six when my family and I moved from a small lake in northern Minnesota to a suburb of Minneapolis. On the lake, we lived in a 400-square-foot house halfway between Aitkin (population 1,000) and Garrison (population 202). Even though there was an extreme amount of violence in my family, when I lived up north I knew something about myself. I belonged somewhere—to the woods and the lake and the trees. My friends were the Pekin and mallard ducks, my collie puppy, and the neighbor's tawny cat. I caught sunnies off our dock and collected them in a steel bucket. I talked to them as they swam circles, fed them chunks of white bread, and then dumped them all back into the lake. I played in the mass of bright orange poppies as tall as I. I listened to the bobcat howl on the frozen lake at night, entranced yet fearful that it would eat Rascal, my puppy, who lived next to the garage in a hay- and snow-packed igloo. There weren't many other children (or adults) in the area and I spent most of my time by myself. But I was not lonely.

When I was a child the wilderness was my home, while the house I lived in was something to escape. My mother and I survived my father's and his friends' beatings, rapes, and verbal assaults in a variety of wood-and-plaster structures throughout rural and suburban Minnesota, but we never really had a home—a place of safety and refuge. Oddly enough, I have been obsessed with owning a house since I was nineteen years old, one with a yard to grow a garden and sit out in while the sun set. I think I was interested in buying a house because once I got away from my father, I realized I could live in a way that I had never known growing up. A house became symbolic of a home, of knowing who I was, of belonging somewhere, having roots.

I spent my twenties in poverty and the thought of ever owning a home seemed unattainable. Living on the verge of homelessness was my reality and actually becoming homeless was a much more likely event than making payments on a Tudor. But in St. Paul I left poverty by working as a massage therapist at Juut Salon. My dream became a full-blown obsession, as much based on the fear of being out in the streets as it was based on the hopes of belonging somewhere. I decided even though I couldn't buy a house at that time, I could get one on a contract-for-deed until I was able to buy it outright. I searched the metropolitan newspapers, found one, and moved into a miniature one-bedroom pea green house in north Minneapolis. The yard was mud. A person could barely stand in the bathroom. There was a drug dealer with two pit bulls across the street. But there was a detached garage, no one from another apartment snoring on the floor above, and the Theo Wirth Parkway was two blocks away—a good place to run the dog and find the land inside the city.

I thought I'd found a home. But I was wrong. My partner and I were splitting apart, the house was miniscule and over-priced by about $40,000. My mother lent me some cash she came into from the sale of her house, I found a Realtor and a broker who were willing to work with my abysmal credit, and I moved one mile south to a slightly larger house with a fenced-in grass yard that I bought for $60,000 less. It was one of the cheapest houses in all of the Twin Cities. It was trashed, smelled like a barn, and had cobwebs the size of my head. A small lake formed in the basement when it rained. Two inches of dust blanketed the woodwork and the tops of the pictures the previous tenants had left on the walls. Even my dog was disgusted by the dust. The first time I pulled down the yellowed lace curtains, he jumped on them enthusiastically, but stopped immediately when dust billowed out, causing us both to sneeze repeatedly. He let me carry them out alone after that.

But the house was mine. After fourteen years of searching, I'd bought a house in my hometown. I expected I would live there for the rest of my life. The land, city, and people were familiar, there was a writing and art scene that was second only to New York, and there was cold and lots of snow.

For two years I worked part-time as a massage therapist, cleaned and remodeled the house, accompanied my mother to her chemotherapy treatments, and attended graduate school. Then my relationship ended, my dog was almost nabbed one night from the backyard, my art burned, and my mother died. My home wasn't safe any longer. I was a mess—devastated, depressed, and lonely.

The night after my art burned I had a dream. A blackened, charred man stepped out of the still-smoldering carcass of a building on Cedar and 16th. He lurched toward me, a blue light flashing like a siren atop his head, then veered off to the right and disappeared into the crowd. In the dream, I felt he was looking for me. I feared that as he lunged about he would see me. Accidentally run into me. Grab me and drag me down, back into the building from which he'd escaped. But he didn't. He disappeared and I was left with dread, sweating in the dark in my house, fervently wishing an Indian woman would call. I flicked on all my lights, sat in bed with my cats and dog, electrified by terror. It was one in the morning. The phone rang. It was my friend, Sam, from the art show. She said she'd had a feeling she should call me. She is eagle clan. I told her what happened. She cried, said I'd better get up there right away.

"Up there" was the White Earth reservation, where Sam lived, healing from years of sexual violence, homelessness, and the violence of being adopted by a Greek family when she was young and then raised as a Greek girl. She didn't know she was Anishinaabe until she was twenty-seven years old. I had plans to visit her in a few months, after things settled down with my mother's death. I would see an Indian doctor, get my Indian name, and watch TV with Sam until three in the morning. But she said to get up there right away, and so I did.

The next weekend my dog and I trundled up Highway 94 over slick black ice roads. Around St. Cloud it began to snow. A bit farther north it became a whiteout and the roads closed. I kept driving, weaving between the ROAD CLOSED signs posted on the heavy metal gates that the state troopers dragged across the highways. I ignored the advice of a Super Motel 8 employee who told me to wait it out at her hotel, used the bathroom and dashed out the front door. I was headed toward something; I was driving away from something. I had to get to Sam's. Blizzard or no blizzard.

I have Indian ancestry on both sides of my family. I was not raised with anything traditional; my grandmothers rarely talked about being part Indian. They were fearful and unsure. They were ashamed. The most my family would say was, "Yeah. We're part Cherokee. Pass the butter." No one said much of anything else about it. The result was that virtually all ties in my family to being Indian were severed and no one knew what to do or think about the connection, so most of us ignored it.

Except me. When I was four, in the woods of northern Minnesota, I wanted to run away, find the Indians, and live with them. I remember being young, settled into the deep backseats of cars when Cher's song about the Cherokee would slide out of the speakers. If there was no one in the backseat with me, I would silently cry. If there was someone, I would fight back the tears, sadness welling up inside me as deep and as long as Mille Lacs Lake, the enormous waterway that nips

Garrison on the lake's north side and runs along an Anishinaabe reservation on the west side.

Later, when we moved to a suburb of Minneapolis, I would
stand between two bathroom mirrors to catch my profile.
What I saw—flat cheeks, round face, and full lips—was startling
and I would quickly turn away as if I had flashed a card in a
poker game that I was supposed to keep hidden. I am light-
skinned, but nonetheless I had those experiences, that
awareness, as a child. In my bones, or maybe my DNA, I knew
I was different from the other girls in the suburb—those blond,
blue-eyed, pointy-faced girls who cared about things I didn't
understand and didn't care about the things I understood.

I couldn't see more than ten feet in front of me; the snow
pelted my windshield and clouded my headlights. My dog was
seat-belted in the jump seat. No one knew where I was; I had
no cell phone; I could have gone off the road at any moment.
No one was traveling, not even the cops. But the time had come
to find out if I could be Indian. I had been hiding those feelings,
that profile, that identity all my life. I'd spent the previous four
years arguing over whether I had any right to be Indian. The
time had come to find out if there was another reason—beside
the abuse—that I was never at home in my skin.

I went into the ditch once, but my four-wheel drive pulled
me out, so I drove slower and paid closer attention to the
drifting mounds of snow on the road. Then the snow slowed to
a simmer, and I could see around me. A few dark silhouettes of
trees, an occasional silo and mammoth barn against the
swirling charcoal gray sky. About forty-five minutes from
Mahnomen, where Sam lived, I saw a familiar blue haze flash
through the grayness. I caught my breath. It was the same light
I'd seen on the charred man from my dream.

Sam greeted me at her door, a bowl of buffalo mac in one
hand and a pearly blue and green abalone shell in the other.
She burned sage and cedar. My dog curled up on one of her
blankets and I relaxed on the couch. Just being in her apartment, the smell of the smudge and the food, put me at ease,
reminded me of a home I'd never known, but had traveled
many roads to find.

The next evening, Sam and I headed out for Earl and
Kathy's house. Sam is blind in one eye and I had never been to

White Earth. On White Earth you can drive for hours and never pass a convenience store or gas station. The only light is from the stars and moon. We took a right instead of a left and became lost on the rural roads, arriving two hours after we told them we would. We had to stop three times, asking for Earl and Kathy's until we found a family who knew them and gave us directions. Earl and Kathy, being on Indian time, did not seem to mind our tardiness, and welcomed us into their home in Naytauwash. Kathy set down cups of black coffee while Earl fried up pancakes. Sam had told me in the car to say "*bungee*," which means "a little," when Earl offered me food or I would have a stack of pancakes high as the ceiling on my plate. It would be rude if I didn't eat what he gave me.

The four of us sat at their table in the kitchen and ate. I passed Earl some *asema*, told him I needed help. Sam made conversation about a variety of things unrelated to me and our visit, while I did my best to eat. The fire had set off terror from my childhood—on the loose were old feelings of being told not to "tell" and the subsequent threats that, if I did, I would be hurt. I couldn't contain them anymore. The night before I'd had a dream that my father and other men were chasing me through the woods. I ran, dodging tree trunks thick as my waist, swiping at undergrowth with my hands. They were just about to grab me when I plunged out of the woods and saw a chasm. I kept running, didn't stop to think, and flew over the chasm, which I knew, at that time in my dream, my father and his men were not allowed to cross. While I was in the air, I turned and I laughed at them. They shot at me. I landed on the other side, the Indian side, and set off into the woods. The dream had a good ending. It was defiant. I escaped. But it was unsettling, too, as precursors of great change always are.

Kathy was quiet, sipping her coffee. Sam talked on. Earl laughed and occasionally said, "Oh," and, "Ah-hah," in his lilting Anishinaabe accent. I said nothing, hunched in a chair across from Kathy, the refrigerator behind me and the stove with a cast iron frying pan cooling to my left. Fourteen months of my mother's cancer. The fire. My life-long feeling of not belonging anywhere. The years of rape and battery and the stress of the unknown about the ceremony I was about to go through. What would Earl say? What would he do? What would happen in the ceremony? I was there to get my

Indian name, that's all I knew. All those feelings surfaced, bubbled, burst out.

My thoughts heaved. I did not belong. I did belong. Maybe I could get help, real help, not Band-Aid therapy. I could not get help. I was "unhelpable." I was Indian. I was not Indian. I was self-conscious, terrified, jumpy. I was out in the middle of the woods—five hours and one snow storm away from Minneapolis. I did not know Kathy and Earl; I was nearly crying; I needed help more than anything. My feelings and thoughts swung like a kids' carousel. Run. Stay. Up. Down. Belong. Don't belong. Round and round.

At some point I knew Earl was waiting for me to do something. I imagined thanking each of them individually and the second I thanked Earl, the last one, he stood up and said, "We're ready." I followed them, one of Sam's skirts pulled on and up over my ragged jeans, through the living room, down a short hall into a bedroom they used for the ceremony.

I cannot write about what happened in the ceremony, but suffice it to say I was nervous. I trembled throughout it. Ceremony is raw, intense, beautiful, and powerful beyond words. It reaches inside you, connecting parts of yourself you never knew existed with the land, trees, water, stones, and all of life. It connects you with your ancestors and their way of life before the Europeans came. It connects you with a vibrant, contemporary Anishinaabe life. I barely breathed; all I wanted was to make it through the ceremony without screwing it up. I did. Earl gave me my Indian name, and Sam and I drove through the dark woods to her apartment. Soon, I returned to Minneapolis.

Three weeks later my mother's bowel became blocked and she died unexpectedly. I went back to White Earth for more ceremonies, more healing, more belonging, more connecting. That summer I worked part-time and spent the rest of my free time up north, making new friends, helping with Defeat Diabetes Day at the Anishinaabe Center, and dancing in the White Earth pow wow. On my way home from the pow wow my car quit right outside of Detroit Lakes. I sat back and said, "Okay, *manidoog,* what now?" I ended up at an acquaintance's house where I spent the next several days waiting for my car.

Donna, who lived in the basement, and I hit it off immediately. We talked, ate at the Chinese Dragon (the one nonchain restaurant in town), and walked her friend's dog, which is part wolf, along the lakeshore. I felt a deep connection with her and we began dating. I had already decided to move near White Earth after graduation, having been told that White Earth is my home, and I belong on it and to it. It felt that way to me.

The summer ended and I went back to school. I still struggled with my identity. When I was on White Earth, with other Indian people, I felt Indian. When I was at school or work or just in the city in general, I did not feel Indian. I felt like a poser. I began to feel lost, like I had in Portland and Orlando. I struggled with the color of my skin, even though many of the Indians on White Earth can pass for white. I struggled with not knowing anything about Anishinaabe or Cherokee ways and with my family's confusion. I struggled with white people who think returning to Indian ways is a joke, especially if you're light-skinned. But I never got those attitudes from other Indian people. They accepted me, welcomed me into their community. I danced and feasted and talked alongside Indians with blond hair, brown hair, red hair, and with black hair, dark and shiny as a crow's wing. My experience, at White Earth and at other Indian gatherings, is that most Indians accept the reality of an Indian Diaspora.

Donna and I decided during my last semester of school that we were going to move in together near White Earth. I landed a full-time teaching position at a nearby community college. We managed, with a lot of footwork, good luck, and money from my mother's estate, to buy a house five minutes off the southwest corner of the reservation. We settled into the 1901 brick house that cost as much as my house in Minneapolis, but is three times as large, with a yard big enough for ten gardens. Donna and I set up an entire room just for her photography and my art, which was undergoing a metamorphosis, too. I used to draw dark abstract portraitures of the men who raped me; I began to draw colorful and abstract birds, animals, and trees that reflected the changes occurring in my life.

The small town we moved to was once the border dividing the Anishinaabe and the Dakota, a border created by white men to keep the Indians from quarrelling with each other and disrupting white settlers. The land around our home is at once beautiful and devastating. The patches of dense woods are stunning, teeming with life, thick with *manidoog*, but much of the woods are now gone. In their place is stripped farmland where once the Anishinaabe and animals of all sizes hunted and birthed and played and died.

After moving to White Earth, I began to learn more about Indian ways. I've sat on porches and listened to how difficult it was for my grandmothers' generation to be Indian. How Indians lost housing, land, and jobs just for being Indian. Back then it didn't matter what your skin color was, if you were light-skinned and someone found out you were Indian you could lose everything—your house, your job, your children. You could be raped and beaten. I've listened to Cherokee friends talk about how Cherokees had to instruct their children not to tell anyone they were Indian because white people could take their land. I've listened to how Indians often passed as white, French, or Italian to protect themselves and their families. I've listened to how the government and Christian churches destroyed connections to traditional culture by assimilation, theft of land, boarding schools, and outlawing of Indian religions. I've listened to how Anishinaabe people had to go deep into the bush in order to keep traditional religion alive. How the U.S. government, which gives so much lip service to freedom, outlawed Indian religions until 1978. How all Indians did not get the vote until 1924.

I've also learned how to sew blankets using 4-inch squares, how to feast the *manidoog*, how to do a four directions smudge, and how to cook traditional foods. And most important, I've learned how to respect all of life and give thanks, every day, for all life around me and my life. The more I learn about Anishinaabe ways, the more I understand that no matter what the white world says, I am Indian, inside and out.

Giiwe, I can imagine my Anishinaabe ancestors saying as they watched over me all these years. *Giiwe*, I can imagine them saying as I made yet another move to a different apartment, a different house, a different city, a different state. But I finally figured it out. I have found home inside and out. My ancestors are pleased.

AS I AM:
LETTERS OF IDENTITY

*"I pray you, in your letters, / when you shall these
unlucky deeds relate, / Speak of me as I am; / nothing
extentuate, / Nor set down aught in malice . . ."*

— William Shakespeare, *Othello*, V, ii, 338

Bufferhood: An Autoethnography Emma Sartwell

Valentine and This Difficult World Tilia Klebenov Jacobs

Emma Sartwell graduated from New York University's Gallatin School of Individualized Study with a degree titled "Towards a Subtractive Art Practice," and was awarded the Leo Bronstein Award for outstanding interdisciplinary study. She has been published in numerous journals and magazines, including the *Gallatin Review,* the *Baltimore Sun,* and *Urbanite Magazine.* Her drawings and photographs have been displayed at Theater for a New City, Current Gallery, and the Baltimore Museum of Art. Sartwell lives in Boulder, Colorado, where she is working toward a Masters in Contemplative Religion at Naropa University.

Bufferhood: An Autoethnography

Emma Sartwell

here you go—this is the first thing I have ever written
directly on the computer,
without writing it out in longhand first.
love,
mom

These were the first words of response to starting my autoethnography. I felt almost ashamed; you can't admit to using email in a research paper. Maybe autoethnography is a relatively new field; maybe it's fitting to admit modern technology. But something seems off; autoethnography may just be too indebted to the past for the ethnographer to be fully present.

But it's worth trying; it's worth collecting nuggets of history, and trying to push the exposure of the author's own subjectivity and warping of the stories. The first warping was instructing my mother to type her tale. She had never typed anything directly into the computer; what an irony that what she typed should be a story from a hundred years ago:

I don't know if my grandfather actually threatened an immigration officer.

He was 16, having survived a perilous journey—was it perilous? Did his mother cry?

How do you send your 16 yr old son to America in the year—what year?—assuming he was about 40 when my father, the youngest, was born in 1926, that would have made the year somewhere around 1902. Why

31

leave Lithonia, a land I imagine of dark woods and shadowy lanes, but in reality was the city of Vilna, a center of rabbinic thought, so there would still be lanes, but now winding through the cobblestone paths of the Jewish ghetto. Were there Cossacks, in black boots? Was there screaming, were there fires, was he scared?

Was his threat to patchke—slap, hit—the man at immigration a bit of feigned bravado, an attempt at keeping his own courage? Was he alone? There was a cousin, because the next bit of the story has him yelling across to another line, telling his cousin—"it's Pats," except in that small bit of translation it was written Patz for the cousin, causing two Americanized versions of the Yiddish slapping. He had a big family—where were his sisters, his brothers? The mother and father were brought here later, promises kept, the father a burly rabbi with a red beard, himself taciturn and tough, although my only memory of him is as a small child, being carried in his arms up an endless flight of dark stairs, towards a woman glowing in a white dress, arms wide, smiling, my grandmother, Bubby.

Where was his sister Rachael, who I was named after, the one he stopped talking to, something about money. Wouldn't she lend him money? Why wouldn't she lend him money? Was it the depression, when he had lost everything? A man who bought houses, founded a Jewish cemetery, drove the first model T, surely the kind of man who as a youth might have sworn in his native tongue at a dense official.

How long was the boat ride over? How did they pay for it? Was Pats really the name of the town they were from, so we are not actually descended from anyone who was in the center of rabbinic thought? Where was the cousin who died with a sewing machine on his back, blood in the snow, running, running with a sewing machine. Did that really happen? And then later in his life my grandfather became a tailor himself—I have his can of buttons—but wasn't he selling furs to New York? Did he travel to New York? And they lived above the store—a connection to the long stairs of my memory—but was it a tailorshop? Why did he found a cemetery? Was he a big macher in the synagogue? Was it an investment?

Was it cold when he got here? He must have had a coat; it was cold in Lithuania. Did he even come in to Ellis Island, or was it the Port of Baltimore? Maybe he had people in Baltimore, and that's how he came to east Baltimore, where you had family and cousins living all around, but according to my father, had to walk to school with your older brother to protect you from taunts and threats. Where if you played a game of basketball on the roof of Cross St. Market, you better not win.

My grandfather, Zayde, died when I was 2, probably almost 3, because my sister was born when I was 3, and my father says he was sorry he never told his father about the pregnancy. Is she named after him? Barbara Farrell, the Hebrew Faygalah, little bird; his name was Morris. I remember my Bubby, kind, who apparently plucked her own chickens in east Baltimore, put heated bricks in the beds to keep her children warm, ran down the street with my father in her arms, ran all the way to the hospital, because he had appendicitis. But no, he had appendicitis years later, in the army. Where was the model T? He was the youngest, somewhat sickly.

My Bubby would spit in your palm and then tickle you up your arm; she would give us Nonpareils and Chiclets. Did she learn that game growing up somewhere in a countryside, where she learned to pluck chickens? What did her parents do? She met my grandfather here, in the U.S., both from Lithuania, both making the trip in their teens.

I have one picture of my Zayde's parents. He is sitting; she is standing beside him with her arm on his chair. She looks like she is about to smile at some private joke; he looks intense. They are both dressed in black.

I recently learned that I have many, many cousins in Baltimore, all of them related to my Zayde. We are the children's children of those who came through

immigration, wandering around Baltimore, unknowingly crossing paths, strident or shy, loud or diffident,
not really sure where we got our names.

How implicated am I in this story? Obviously, I have inherited
the questioning syntax. But have I inherited the fear, the
chutzpah, the Old World lore?

I didn't take the name Pats. But I don't feel like a Sartwell,
either—coming over on the Mayflower from England and
Ireland to live in New Hampshire and fight in the wars. The
Sartwells are writers, drinkers, Communists, farmers, teachers.
The Patses are doctors, suburbanites, eaters and yakkers. I feel
like a Sartwell personally, but the lineage is foreign; something
is off—I'm just not that *white*.

Really? I check the Caucasian box on forms; I feel guilt at
the thought of slavery or Whites Only bathrooms; I never
consciously feel that my race is a detriment, a consideration,
or much of anything at all. Yet I have been told all my life that
"my people" have been persecuted: *we* built the pyramids; *we*
fled the Inquisition; *we* are the ones to be rooted out by
eugenics. I may be white, but I'm certainly not Aryan; I may
have no room to complain about the status of my ethnicity in
this country; but a master race wouldn't want anyone so hairy
and olive. These "my people" are not the blue-eyed Sartwells.
Could my feelings of distance from the Puritans be simply a
chasm in time? Or does it have something to do with all the
Passover seders and family bar mitzvahs?

> o.k. sorry we missed you at the seder maybe next
> year
> love zayde
> we lived in a non-jewish neighborhood and my
> zayde lived with us. he had a long white beard and
> whenever we walked outside the kids would always
> shout "here comes Santa Claus" regardless of the
> season. more next time.

Richard Dyer says that "there is something especially white in
this non-located and disembodied position of knowledge" (4).
That's what I'm doing at NYU, honing my disembodied position
of knowledge. I copied that note out of my Gmail, and am now

thinking about the post-structuralist implications of my grand-father's capitalization. Maybe that mode of automatic analysis can be attributed to our culture's "white" priorities, which are inevitably re-produced in its liberal arts colleges. In fact, white-ness may be having less and less to do with race, more and more to do with class and education. A private university instills ideals that could be called "white," but are only tangen-tially connected to skin color. But I think my "whiteness" runs deeper than that; I think it is ingrained in me by more than society: it's in my bones, my childhood, my subconscious. I yearn to analyze in the cold lineage of the white man. It's the white man who finds himself provoking reactions; the brown man doesn't have to. It's the white man who romanticizes self-destruction; the yellow man has plenty of people to do it for him. It's the white man who has a hard time finding commu-nity, and is left dealing with his mind and his word processor.

Three summers ago, I tattooed a semicolon on my wrist. Both of my parents were upset. My mom had her reasons, and as a mother, seeing your daughter grow up is understandably troubling. But part of her anxiety seemed to stem from an attachment to Jewish code: You can't be buried in a Jewish cemetery with tattoos. My dad was angry because he had wanted to get a matching tattoo, a colon, and now we couldn't do it together. My dad's immediate family is buried in a small circle (a diameter of maybe twelve feet) of land on my grand-mother's farm in Virginia. On so many levels, I am a Sartwell.

Perhaps again my self-definition is a re-production of soci-etal or archetypal expectations. I have assumed the rationale of my *father* and the physicality of my *mother*. In his book *The Alphabet Versus the Goddess*, Leonard Shlain articulates the divide between "male" and "female" (as a symbolic duality): "a *holistic, simultaneous, synthetic*, and *concrete* view of the world are the essential characteristics of a feminine outlook; *linear, sequential, reductionist,* and *abstract* thinking defines the masculine" (1). Dyer's view of whiteness echoes Shlain's view of the masculine: "The notion of whiteness having to do with tightness, with self-control, self-consciousness, mind over body" (6). I feel the tightness.

No matter how much you value mind over body, though, you can't escape your body, and others are particularly bound to experience your body before your mind. And what a strange time to be a Jewess! In the Lower East Side, it's a wonderful commodity to have. It's your ticket into Heeb readings, Yiddish theater, and work-study positions revolving around matzah sculptures. Eating falafel doesn't feel like co-opting someone else's culture, and everyone's always trying to take you to Israel for free.

> Dear Emma—
> As well as I can remember here is my recall of the egg game, I grew up in a non-Jewish neighborhood. At Easter time the kids would come outside with raw eggs and yell "whos gotta egg" when one of their friends would respond they would crack their eggs against each other—points to points and butts to butts. The one whose egg got cracked in the process would have to give it to the one whose egg did not crack. The winner would take the cracked eggs home and decorate it for Easter. At Passover we use hard boiled eggs and crack them against each other's eggs. The one who has the last uncracked egg is the winner (champion). Then we eat the eggs as an appetizer.
> Love Zayde

For the second time, my Zayde refers to his neighborhood as "non-Jewish." I'm assuming this means "white." At the very least, it suggests a feeling of separateness; there are Jewish communities and non-Jewish communities, and that sounds a lot like a racial barrier. A Jew living in a non-Jewish neighborhood (in the first half of the twentieth century), though, would presumably have had a much easier time than a black person in a non-black neighborhood. This may reinforce Dyer's idea of "buffer" people, those near-whites who act as cushion "between the white and the black or indigenous" (19). It occurs to me that the difference between Jewish and non-Jewish may be mostly conceptual: Who has accepted Jesus? Who plays egg games on Easter and who on Passover? But that can't be the whole story: My family has worried about accepting non-Jews into the mix. And the implication is that our race is more in danger of bleaching out because of our "buffer" status. We have to remain distinct. My mother writes:

there's the story of introducing blond, blue-eyed
crispin—(did you say christian?)
to my family—
raised anti-religion by a lapsed catholic and a secular jew,
(religion is a crutch for the weak, you know)
anyway, when my parents pressed on, and found out his
mother was actually jewish oh, how great!
you are a non-practicing jew! my mother announced,
(much to crispin's surprise)
and then it was all right.

And then there's the story that she can't really remember
about a woman in Alabama (where we were living at the time)
who asked if she could see my mother's horns.

Here's the crux: I feel guilty expressing racial pride because
I receive so many of my culture's white benefits. I feel "the
problem of 'me-too-ism,'" that Dyer refers to as "a feeling that,
amid this (*all* this?) attention being given to non-white subjects,
white people are being left out" (10). While Dyer says these feelings need to be "guarded against," I think they should merely
be exposed. Most likely, one of my reasons for collecting family
stories is that I feel left out. I want a history that rivals Zora
Neale Hurston's, even though—no, *because* it was my people
who dragged her people across an ocean in chains, leaving
them with not much more than their stories. These feelings are
crucial to whiteness.

I have the luxury of saying "my people" were oppressors,
and "my people" were oppressed. By putting together an
autoethnography, we get to romanticize, exoticize, and validate
ourselves. Cultural theorist Susan Stewart says that

> the exotic object is to some degree dangerous, even
> "hot." Removed from its context, the exotic souvenir
> is a sign of survival—not its own survival, but the
> survival of the possessor outside his or her own context
> of familiarity. Its otherness speaks to the possessor's
> capacity for otherness: it is the possessor, not the
> souvenir, which is ultimately the curiosity. (148)

In an autoethnography, the stories are the souvenirs. We
lay them out for people to see, and we say, "I survived this!

My people came over on a cold boat when they were four!" It makes sense that the stories ethnographers seem to be attracted to are in themselves about dangerously acquiring souvenirs: keeping Pats, for example, after threatening to slap the immigration officer in the face. To place oneself in the realm of otherness through stories is a safe way to complicate and add interest to one's self-definition: the souvenir "los[es] its specific referent and eventually point[s] to an abstracted otherness that describes the possessor" (Stewart 148). On a campus of whiteness, in the detached world of academia, it's more and more desirable to be distinct, to relate to a "primitivism" that's both before and beyond research papers. And by displaying/displacing our "primitive" souvenirs in an intellectual context, we heighten their significance: "For the invention of the exotic object to take place, there must first be separation. It must be clear that the object is estranged from the context in which it will be displayed as a souvenir; it must be clear that use value is separate from display value" (149).

> here you go—this is the first thing I have ever
> written directly on the computer,
> without writing it out in longhand first.
> love,
> mom

Most of my family's stories have never been written down. Most I have never heard explicitly told, only referred to year after year: "The souvenir is destined to be forgotten; its tragedy lies in the death of memory, the tragedy of all autobiography and the simultaneous erasure of the autograph" (151). Most of them aren't true.

I have exoticized myself. I am exoticized by the world. Undoubtedly those two actions rely on each other.

I am non-white and I am white. I have a culture that gives me access to the sufferers and access to the powerful. I am sometimes left dangling in between. I have a collection of stories.

SOURCES

Richard Dyer. *White*. New York: Routledge, 2002. 1–40. Print.

Rachael K. Gardner. Email interview. Apr. 2007.

Albert Pats. Email interview. Apr. 2007.

Leonard Shlain. *The Alphabet Versus the Goddess*. New York: Penguin, 1999. Print.

Susan Stewart. *On Longing*. Durham: Duke UP, 1993. Print.

Tilia Klebenov Jacobs lives in Framingham, Massachusetts. While growing up she traveled extensively, due to her father's position with the U.S. State Department, and she lived on three continents before her twelfth birthday. As a child, she spoke only Spanish, and her awareness of cultural issues was further heightened by the fact that her father was Jewish and her mother, Episcopalian. Klebenov Jacobs attended Oberlin College, where she majored in religion and English with a concentration in creative writing. She went on to earn a Master of Theological Studies from Harvard Divinity School and a secondary school teaching certification from the Harvard Graduate School of Education. While in graduate school she converted to Judaism. She continues to explore the richness of cultures and the areas where minority and majority mindsets intersect and collide. Klebenov Jacobs's awards include the Linda Joy Myers Memoir Prize and honorable mention in the Dorothy Churchill Cappon Essay Award from *New Letters*. Her work has been published in *The Jewish Magazine*, *WILLA*, and in *Phoenix Rising: Collected Papers on Harry Potter* (2008). She teaches writing in two Massachusetts prisons.

Valentine and This Difficult World

Tilia Klebenov Jacobs

I had heard about this letter but had never seen it.

It is postmarked August 7, 1957, and addressed to my mother in an elegant, Victorian hand. The occasion of the letter is my parents' engagement. The author is my grandmother, and the subject of the letter is the sticky subject of my father's Semitic origins. Put succinctly, my father was Jewish and my mother wasn't.

When I say "wasn't," one must strain to imagine the almost impossible depths of wasn'tness in this regard. My mother was Mary Langdon Elwyn Mitchell Gammell of East Greenwich, Rhode Island. She always went by Elwyn: Ellie when she was younger, Els to her inner circle. Her father's family founded her home state in 1636 (it became official in 1644); never a gang to rest on their laurels, they went on to establish Brown University in 1764 and to sign the Declaration of Independence in 1776. Her father was a veteran of World War I, following which he became a successful financier.

My maternal grandmother's family was no less distinguished. They hailed from Philadelphia and included physician Weir Mitchell, an eminent pre-Freudian psychiatrist and the first person to discover the sympathetic nervous system; and Langdon Mitchell, a well-known playwright in his day. My grandmother herself, one Susanna Valentine Mitchell Gammell by name, was a successful novelist. She published under the name Mitchell, but was Valentine to friends and family.

In short, my mother's was a prominent and successful family. With ancestors like that, how could they be anything else? My mother was the second of three children, with older sister Helena Hope and younger brother Arthur Middleton ("Midd"). The former was named in part for the daughter of Roger Williams, the aforementioned founder of Rhode Island; the latter, for the ancestral signer of the Declaration. All of them knew with brilliant conviction that they could do everything and anything they ever wanted to do in life.

That generation of Gammells belonged to a class of people that was more common five or six decades ago than today, and as such they are rather difficult to describe. Perhaps the best comparison would be to the stars of old movies. The Gammell men were as elegant as Cary Grant. The women had the poise of Lauren Bacall. Everyone was erudite; everyone was witty; and the entire family radiated a kind of hearty Episcopalianism. (One might reasonably conclude that Protestantism originated with them.) The Gammells had a robust elegance that is rare now; they viewed the world as their personal oyster, shucked just for them.

I think the Gammells' blithe confidence in their own superiority is typified by my mother's approach to her education. She and her sister attended the Foxcroft School in the forties; and with all due respect to Foxcroft, which I am sure has changed tremendously in the past seventy years, they both loathed it. (Interestingly, a 1942 letter from the headmistress of that school to my apparently jittery grandmother assures her that Foxcroft has no Jews. Imagine her relief.)

Following her high school experience, my mother decided not to attend college, not out of any lack of ambition or intellect but because she judged that she was already highly educated and would continue to read and learn for the rest of her life. This being the case—and it was a fair assessment—what could formal education offer her?

Ultimately my mother did go to college; a relative took her aside and explained that, intellect or no, her life would be easier if she earned a degree. So she attended the University of Pennsylvania for two years, then finished at Barnard.

If the Gammell men were Grantish, I think it is fair to say there was something Hepburnesque about my mother. She was equal parts gusto and refinement, doing what she wanted and doing it well. Having served her four-year sentence in the halls of higher education, my mother was now free to do exactly as she pleased; so looking not much like Audrey but sounding quite a bit like Katharine, in 1955 my mother went off to Paris. There was no reason not to.

There she crossed paths with my father, one Eugene Klebenov of Cohasset, Massachusetts. He was an impecunious Jew born of immigrant parents, and he took one look at her and fell madly in love.

I have always felt that there was a certain cachet to the fact that my parents met at a sidewalk café in Paris, and indeed I have long cherished a fantasy that Fred Astaire and Ginger Rogers were seated at the next table. The whole thing is just so darned romantic. In any case, it was at its inception a giddy and joyful union. One of the only flies in the proverbial ointment was breaking the news to my mother's parents that their bluestocking daughter was marrying a gentleman whose fortunes were not yet made, and who was decidedly not Christian.

Lest we slip into cliché, let me hasten to add that in typical immigrant fashion my father's parents and grandparents had worked hard and played by the rules of their adopted country, and as a result had done well for themselves. When telling family stories, my father always made it clear that his grandparents, who came to our shores during the vast wave of European immigration of the 1890s, were not fleeing oppression in the stereotypical sense of the term. In other words, no hordes of Cossacks or burning synagogues appeared in their metaphorical rearview mirror; and in any case, they were too busy looking forward to care much about what lay behind them. What propelled them was, quite simply, the promise of a better life in America. "They were economic refugees," my father always said, "not religious ones." They came here for opportunity, then went about creating it for themselves.

My great-uncle Mark, the first of his family to arrive, disembarked in New York. My understanding is that like most immigrants of the era he could carry all his possessions with one hand. His family had been farmers in the Old Country, and apparently successful ones at that; but they knew they could do better in America. It almost goes without saying that he didn't speak English and had no money to speak of.

The man taught himself how to read at the New York Public Library. He must have spoken both Russian and Yiddish, so English was his third language—and, it should be noted, his third alphabet. He got a job; he worked hard; he made enough money to send for his family. They came with babes in arms. One of them was my grandfather.

A few years later my grandmother arrived the same way. Her family had been tailors, not farmers, and they were from a different part of Russia. Otherwise the stories are similar enough and the mindset identical: if, as Jews, they could be moderately prosperous in Russia, imagine what they could do as Americans!

And so they did.

My grandfather's family founded a successful candy company by the name of American Nut Co. (No jokes, please— it's too easy.) Quite rapidly they morphed into successful, middle-class citizenship, owning their own homes and taking the standard vacations and holidays. My grandmother's family did the same.

Both of my paternal grandparents claimed to have been born in the United States; my grandmother knew better, but my grandfather may genuinely have believed it to be true. In either case the assertion speaks volumes about their feelings for their country. They were Americans, pure and simple.

An indicator of their success was my father's career in the world. Despite coming from parents whose formal education stopped after high school, my father was educated at Thayer and Harvard, a man of impressive and far-ranging intellect. Like my mother, though unlike his now firmly rooted parents, he decided early on that the world was a tableau of opportunities, his to explore. After he had served a stint in the army in the early 1950s, he found himself honorably discharged and in Paris; and that is where my mother took one look at him and fell in mutual mad love with him.

Though their courtship unfurled in Paris, their engagement was precipitated by events back home. In August 1956, the ocean liner *Andrea Doria* foundered off the coast of New England while en route to Europe. My mother had been scheduled to take that ship back home from France. When the ship sank, Mom was stranded on the Continent for a few extra days. Taking advantage of the opportunity, my father proposed and my mother said yes.

And now we come to the letter from my grandmother.

My parents were wed in 1958, when the intermarriage rate among Jews hovered around 13 percent. The number of Episcopalians marrying Jews must have been microscopic. As a result, this was a Big Deal, at least for my mother's family. (Interestingly, my father's family appears to have been both silent and sanguine about the match.) My grandmother's letter was written almost a year before my parents tied the knot, and Granny was distinctly uneasy about the whole thing.

"I am troubled about Eugene," she confides. "I think New York a good idea but even then unless he, as an agnostic, is willing to put his race behind him—he is after all an American—I see lifelong difficulties."

What sort of difficulties? They are never spelled out, but they don't need to be. They are of the anti-Semitic sort, and for this reason my grandmother didn't want anyone to know my father was Jewish. She did not object to the marriage itself—indeed, she supported it—but she most decidedly did not want Society to know The Truth.

It was the fifties, after all. Anti-Semitism was as acceptable a prejudice as homophobia is today. The 1950s were a time of conformity, spelled WASP, and pressure to conform breeds intolerance for those who can't or won't. Fortunately, however, Granny had a solution, a simple step my father could take that would fix everything.

Ready? It's a doozy.

He ought to change his name legally to Clayburne, and never admit to anyone that he has Jewish blood.

Granny's anxiety and problem-solving skills churn to a crescendo as she considers what might lie ahead socially for my parents. She urges my mother to use all her influence on my father to get him to take a position with Raytheon, a company where my grandfather had considerable clout—having been one of its founders. She is clearly baffled at what she sees as the younger generation's penchant for creating difficulties when a smattering of decorous obfuscation could clear them right up.

> [W]hy not a job with E. Spenser or Raytheon? You could live in Prov[idence], have a position as a Gammell, and a far easier time (since you want a large family) than in New York. Or is Eugene bent on making difficulties, and does he refuse any but the self-created opportunities? Believe me, in this difficult world one needs all the help one can get.

It sounds pretty bad, admittedly. The directive to change his name is, though lovingly put, draconian; and to our post-Holocaust ears the reference to "Jewish blood" is cringeworthy at least, nauseous at worst. Thus we now arrive at the critical question: Was my Granny anti-Semitic?

And the answer that comes to me is no. At least not in the way that most people might think. Certainly there was no malice in her observations; in the same letter she describes my father as "sweet" and "very dear." Furthermore, and more tellingly, she urges my mother to marry him lickety-split rather than indulge in a long engagement; for, as she observes with what may be a hint of roguishness, "engagements that go on too long do not always come off." Not only was Eugene Klebenov good enough for Elwyn Gammell, but the time to act was now. Clearly this is far from a classic case of not wanting her daughter to marry one.

So if it wasn't typical anti-Semitism, what was it? My grandmother thought highly of my father, and wanted the marriage to happen without delay. So why did she urge my mother to "never mention the word Jew in connection with him to anyone at all, not even to me"? (Seems a little silly, doesn't it? Was she hoping it might later slip her mind, leaving the spot labeled "Gene's socioreligious background" pleasantly vacant?)

Well, several factors come into play. One was my grandmother's age. She was sixty-one when she penned that letter, meaning she was born in 1896. She was seven in 1903 when the Wright Brothers flew their first plane at Kitty Hawk; twenty-four in 1920 when the first radio station opened. She was ten in 1906 when the secret police of the Czar of Russia published a vitriolic forgery titled *The Protocols of the Elders of Zion*, and twenty-four when Henry Ford (yes, *the* Henry Ford) published the American edition of same with the catchy title *The International Jew: The World's Foremost Problem*. She was thirty-one when Lindbergh flew across the Atlantic in 1927, and in her mid-forties when that same Lindbergh founded the America First Movement, which attempted to prevent U.S. involvement in World War II by claiming that Jews sought it in their own interests and against America's.

When my grandmother was growing up, and indeed when she was raising her children, many respectable neighborhoods wouldn't allow Jews. Private schools catered to wealthy Christians and part of their mission was making sure the children of same met the right people, who were also wealthy and Christian. Two world wars and a Holocaust separated my grandmother's twenties from my mother's. It was a staggeringly different world, and surely she was not wrong to fear the poison of the prejudices that surrounded her when she herself was growing up.

Thus, much of what she said in the letter was true.

I don't want your children injured, and even Jews with great fortunes undergo great difficulties. A poor Jew is forgiven nothing. But absolute silence so that none of your friends know will help—and I believe a change of name would be a further aid, and this before the engagement is in the Press. If he were a devout Jew I would shrug and accept with regret. He is not. And a change of name deprives him of neither church nor nationality. But discretion, my child, is all-important.

I am sure she was right that wealthy Jews were blamed for much. Certainly she was even more correct that a poor Jew is forgiven nothing.

She is also not wrong to describe my father as less than devout. In fact, this was if anything an understatement so deft as to resemble sleight of hand. If Protestantism was based on my mother's family, then my father's way of life defined new horizons in the art of Jewish nonobservance. I was in my twenties before I saw him darken the door of any Jewish establishment, and even that was all but unavoidable, since it was a funeral home on the occasion of a death in his family. When I say he did not observe the holidays, I mean that he never knew when they occurred. He never denied his Judaism, but he never partook of it, either.

Of course none of that matters to an anti-Semite. As any minority can attest, we can never assimilate enough to please the people who hate us. So my grandmother was not wrong when she said that my mother's yet-to-be-born children would have an "easier" time if no one knew they were half Jewish—though by the time we were all growing up in the seventies I can honestly say it was a nonissue.

And here is the most mitigating factor of all: my grandmother was mentally ill when she wrote the letter.

I do not know the name of the incubus that robbed her of her sanity in her adult years; I know that it came and went in unpredictable cycles. I have heard competing theories of schizophrenia and bipolarism. The formal diagnosis is irrelevant, as it would most likely be given a different name today. All I know is that she was delusional, though not reliably so. As a result it is impossible to tease out her prejudices from her illness; but whenever I come across something particularly loopy in her correspondence, I tend to chalk it up to the latter. Nor am I alone in this. Witness the opening paragraph from a letter to my parents from my aunt Helena Hope:

3 January 1962

Dearest Mango and Papaya,

First, while I think of it, please check to see that Ma is still taking her Pills and seeing Dr. Lebensohn when necessary. Her recent spate of letters to me re Midd's travels seem to have lost all sense of proportion—and have some pretty silly ideas about how civilized the Soviets are in comparison with the rest of the bloc countries. (She appears to be under the impression that the ability to handle a cocktail glass in company is

the equivalent of an agreement with the principles of
Life, Liberty and the Pursuit of Happiness. It ain't!)

Let me hasten to add that I have no idea why Helena Hope
referred to my parents by names of tropical fruits. My best
guess is that it was her version of Mamma and Papa. Like all
good Gammells, she was addicted to wordplay, large and small.
In any case, the point here is that Granny's instability and—I'm
being kind here—quirky view of the world were a well-known
commodity.

Finally, Granny was a busybody. Her own sister, my great-
aunt Sissie, summed up Granny's personality in a 1964 letter to
my mother as follows. One can imagine tongue lovingly
inserted in cheek throughout.

> I'm sure [your mother] had a fine Christmas. Has she
> made a devout Christian of Gene yet? And no doubt a
> perfect man in many ways. . . . She wouldn't really be
> herself if she weren't trying to reform us all and each a
> trifle one way or another.

But back to 1957. What's a young couple to do? They can't
hope to change the social codes around them, at least not in
time for the wedding. But perhaps they could at least put
Granny's letter to rest. Much like Sissie, they knew the best way
to deal with Granny was with love and humor. In this they were
aided by a finely honed sense of the absurd. So rather than
spend her nights howling, "Why art thou Klebenov?" my
mother shared the letter with my father.

And how did my father respond to this goofiness, this
bigotry, this intimation that *I* don't object but you know how
people are?

Upon having digested the contents of the missive he sat
down and penned a reply to my grandmother in which he
gravely explained to her that he had read her letter and given
her concerns due consideration; and although he had over the
years grown fond of "Klebenov" with its cavalcade of consonants that rolled trippingly off the tongue, he could not deny
the logic of her observations. Therefore, he concluded, he
would indeed change his name, to . . .

. . . wait for it . . .

. . . wait . . .

Von Resnik.

My mother wouldn't let him send it, though I have no doubt she mined the heartiest of belly laughs from its pages.

In any event, my parents did get married.

I have only one snapshot of May 30, 1958. It was a breezy day, to judge by the way my mother's back-hanging veil is blowing in the breeze, and sunny. She and my father are standing by the bushes outside my grandfather's back porch. My father's arm is around her shoulder, and he is gazing down at her in awe. He being a full foot taller than she, her neck is craned to gaze up at him. The light shines more fully on her face than his, so I can see her smile clearly.

They both look exuberantly happy.

Mrs. Gammell
3028 Cambridge Place, N.W.
Washington 7, D.C.

Oct. 11, 1962

Dear Gene,

I should have sat down and written this letter yesterday, when I had it all in mind. Now I've set up a road block, and it will be only half the letter I meant it to be.

It's chiefly to tell you how glad I am Elwyn married <u>you</u>. Not someone else. And not only because she's so deeply in love with you. But because you're the kind of man you are. I've always liked you since the evening you were introduced to me, but now I have a constant confidence in you, and an affection that I don't like to express because it makes it seem unreal. Well, it isn't.

Go on taking care of her, and take care of yourself.

Much love,
Valentine

THE TONGUE OF WAR:
A CLASH OF CULTURES

> *"I see on an immense scale . . . that disease, wars, the unloosened, devastating elemental forces have each and all played their part in developing and hardening man and giving him the heroic fiber."*

— John Burroughs (1837–1921), *Accepting the Universe*, 1922

Reflecting on Dragons and Angels Shanti Elke Bannwart

Tongue-Tied Kelly Hayes-Raitt

Tightrope Across the Abyss Shanti Elke Bannwart

Shanti Elke Bannwart was born in Hamburg, Germany, at the onset of World War II. The experience of war during childhood formed her view on life. In 1982, after living in Switzerland and Scotland, she immigrated to the United States to study psychology. Today, Bannwart, in her seventies, lives in Santa Fe, New Mexico, and is a licensed counselor and life-coach, a spiritual seeker and elder, and is devoted to "Reflective Activism" on the issues of war and peace. (She is cofounder of Women for Peace and is a member of Women in Black.) She received an MFA in Creative Writing from Goddard College, and her essays have been published in national and international magazines, including *Pitkin Literary Magazine, The Santa Fe Sun, Aquila, Tokyo Advocate*, and she has been awarded prizes and finalist standing in several national contests. "Reflecting on Dragons and Angels" (excerpted here) also won the SWW Southwest Writers National Contest in 2009, and appears in her memoir, *Dancing on One Foot*, published by Sunstone Press in 2012.

Reflecting on Dragons and Angels

Shanti Elke Bannwart

● ● ● I remember May 8, 1945, when a radio announcement declared the end of World War II. I was six years old and observed how the women of the neighborhood got very busy. They made huge pots of green peppermint tea and bowls full of red berry juice and prepared plates of dry bread and cooked potatoes, whatever scarce food they found in their pantries. The women washed their hair and put lipstick on: They colored the upper lip in the shape of a heart and then they rolled the lower lip against the upper. They smiled and leaned their heads back to pluck their eyebrows into a fine, thin line. They cut their toenails and took colorful dresses off hangers to hold against their figures, turning in front of mirrors that they hadn't looked into for a long time. Some painted with steady hands and eyebrow liner pencil a long black seam from their heels upward to their buttocks to pretend they were wearing silk stockings. My mother fixed a red tulip blossom in her hair.

That morning, we had heard the news about the end of war from the small radio in our kitchen, which was fixed to the wall like a little altar I'd seen in church. It was called *Volksempfänger*—people's radio—and had only one station. It often scratched and moaned like a sick animal, especially when *Der Führer* bellowed his speeches and filled our home with a heavy stench of madness. Carved wood ornaments on the front of the radio covered the brown fabric in the back that trembled when his voice poured out. But today a different speaker announced that the war was over and that the Allied Troops would march into Germany.

War was a backdrop for my childhood, something strange and ever-present for me and I assumed it was a common part of life. War's presence hid in the corners of our home and wafted like a foul stench behind the curtains and underneath my bed, but we did not talk about it. The men were at "the front" and the women carried and sustained life at home in their straight and crooked ways. Nobody explained to me what "end of war" meant, and so many things had already ended before this "end."

In front of our house was a triangle of grass between three merging streets. The women set up their drinks and food in this place, and then we stood and waited. Soon a rhythmic scraping sound rolled toward us; then soldiers of the German army appeared. They moved by the crowd, a seemingly never-ending murky river of men. I stood in front of my mother and held her hand; she wore the blue and white dress that I loved so much. I hadn't seen it on her since the family vacation at the Baltic Sea, years ago. I leaned my head backward against her belly.

The German soldiers lurching in front of us were dirty, wounded, tired, their eyes glazed and their movements helpless and awkward. Some sat on horse-pulled carts, others on bikes, most walked. A man with only one arm and a bandaged hand tried to cling to one of the wagons, but his bloody hand slipped off and he nearly tumbled to the ground. He caught himself and slouched forward. I could smell his sweat.

The women leaned into the street to offer drink and food; I observed the soft, white underside of their arms and chins when I looked up. The soldiers grabbed the gifts hastily. They continued their march as they drank and some sent an exhausted smile back to the person who had extended this gesture of caring. The stream of tired human bodies was pushed by an invisible power toward an invisible goal. There was a feeling of utter futility. It seemed as if they were moving from nowhere to nowhere. Everybody was quiet, as if attending a funeral. Only the boots of the soldiers scratched along the sandy road.

After a long time, the last of the military men dwindled away like dry leaves blown into the corners of our destroyed country. But the women stayed and waited—I didn't know why. And then they came, the next river of men, the English and American soldiers, the occupiers of our burnt earth. They looked clean and shaven; their belts and boots sparkled. They carried healthy limbs and unbroken self-esteem. They smiled at the women who greeted them with the same gestures of lifting their arms with drink and food in their hands, leaning toward the men and exchanging smiles. The women's naked arms reached across me toward the soldiers like flowers to the sun. There were shouts of Hello! and Thank you! The men waved and the women brightened. It seemed that the whole world was sucking in air and exhaling after holding tight, for too long, in a suffocating clench. I wondered if the losing soldiers were the wrong and unworthy ones, and the victors were right, just by the fact that they had won the war. Their prowess and unbrokenness was attractive and seemed to charge up the group of women with electric and glistening desire. I, too, thought that they looked splendid.

I moved the tip of my shoe back and forth in the dust and rocks of the road, back and forth, scraping a little half circle in front of me. What was the meaning of these strange parades? Both—losers and winners—had faces and hands and feet; they looked very similar. Why were some enemies and the others "our people"? And the enemies were so friendly and kind. They gave us children chewing gum, something I had never tasted before. It stuck to my teeth and made my mouth drip with pleasure. It was a miracle food; I could bite and bite on it and it never got smaller. I liked these soldiers; they made me smile. They were not frightening. Were these the men who threw the bombs on my town and burned Hamburg to the ground until the houses looked like rotten teeth?

I held tightly on to my mother's hand as I watched the manly legs marching by in front of me, my eyes at the height of their belts and dangling pistols. I feared if I let go I might fall apart and scatter into pieces, like a puzzle that couldn't be assembled into a whole picture. My head rumbled with all the things stuffed inside that I didn't understand. I was too young to know what I know today, that we were witnessing the last aching gasps of the most widespread war in human history. I didn't know that over seventy million people were killed during six years, most of them civilians like us: women and children. We were standing at the sidelines to watch the last convulsions of the deadliest global conflict ever. The majority of the world's nations had spent their most precious human, economic, and scientific resources on the destruction of human cultures and lives.

We women and children hovered at the edge of the river of men-of-war in front of us; we were standing like a living wall. The soldiers were flowing by, their movements splashing along our hips, our bellies, and our breasts. We were a riverbank with roots and rocks in it and they were the current, whirling and changing the shape of the ground. We had an appointment with history and we knew it in the marrow of this very moment. Out of the corners of our eyes we recognized the slanted landscape of an unknown future. A future when we would sit together and would become quiet and struggle with words and stare out of the windows—holding on tightly to each other's hands. A future when we would say: "Do you remember?" and "It was bad," and "It was good," . . . and so on . . . and so on. . . .

Kelly Hayes-Raitt is the author of several award-winning articles, including "Tongue-Tied," which is the first chapter of her journalistic memoir about work with refugees. A recipient of five writing fellowships, she has lived in writing colonies as far-flung as Bialystok, Poland. She is a college lecturer and a public speaker and divides her time between Los Angeles, California, and Ajijic, Mexico. In July 2003, as she entered Iraq three months after the U.S.-led invasion, Hayes-Raitt was press credentialed by the Jordanian government. She reported live from Baghdad, Fallouja, Hilla, and Basra via satellite phone to NPR, KNBC-TV, and other news outlets. Additionally, she wrote a series of columns for the *Santa Monica Daily Press*. Random House published two of those columns in *Female Nomad & Friends: Tales of Breaking Free and Breaking Bread Around the World* (2010), and "Tongue-Tied" was also included in *The Best Women's Travel Writing 2011*. Since 2007, Hayes-Raitt has reported while held at gunpoint at a checkpoint in the West Bank, from a Palestinian refugee camp a week after the Lebanese Army destroyed it, and from No Man's Land between the Syrian and Iraqi borders. As an independent citizen-journalist, she has been able to slip into places where mainstream reporters are barred.

Tongue-Tied

Kelly Hayes-Raitt

The one I want to wrap in my arms and bring home is Nebras.

I don't even know her name when I return to Iraq, shortly after the assault on Baghdad. I am armed only with a photo of a beggar touching her nose with her tongue.

I had met her a few months before, when I'd traveled to Iraq with a women's delegation, just five weeks before the U.S. bombings and invasion. Unfazed by impending disaster, the little girl, old enough to be in primary school, had begged for handouts in the marketplace *souk*. I had taught her to touch her nose with her tongue. We'd teased; clearly she wasn't used to an adult making faces at her and delighting in her company. She'd followed me around the *souk*, nearly swallowing her tongue in laughter as she imitated my nose-touching stunt.

She was cold. The dirty scarf wrapped loosely around her

neck neither protected her from the chill nor hid her calcu-
lating ability to work the shoppers. Without a translator, the
most I gathered from the encounter was a photo of a gleeful
girl with laughing eyes and an incredibly acrobatic tongue.

When I return to Iraq five months later to find how war has
touched the people who have so deeply touched me, transla-
tors are reluctant to take me to the *souk*. The mood in Baghdad
has shifted; gunfire is heard nightly and no one wants to be
responsible for my harm. Finally, I convince one translator to
take me "shopping." I canvass the cluttered shops for hours,
flashing the little girl's photo.

"Yes, that's Nebras." Finally a shopkeeper recognizes the
girl whose deep brown eyes had humanized the smoldering
CNN newscasts that absorbed my life back home. "But I haven't
seen her in a while. Not since before the war."

I catch my breath. I had just learned Nebras's name. She
can't be one of the thousands of nameless Iraqis we dismis-
sively call "collateral damage." I step out into the bright sunlight
and my translator catches my arm.

"We need to leave," he insists. The equally insistent gunfire
across the river rattles my nerve. I feel conspicuous in the *souk's*
crowded narrow alleys. People dart, avoiding eye contact.
Shops close prematurely. Barricaded soldiers seem hyper-alert
in the edgy heat.

As we worm our way back to our car, I stifle my creeping
panic. Behind me, a commotion suddenly erupts and I turn
around to see a crowd of men shoving toward me. I freeze. The
shopkeepers part, revealing the terrified eyes of a familiar
elfish girl they drag toward me by the scruff of her T-shirt.

Nebras doesn't recognize me at first. Not until I show her
photos of herself does she smile. Backed against a shop facing
a tight crowd of curious men, Nebras retreats shyly, studying
her photo intently. I shoo back the men who had treated this
beggar only as a nuisance and, kneeling before her, I ask the
interpreter to tell her I had come from America to see her.

Without warning, the overwhelmed girl lunges forward
and kisses me on the lips.

We buy her an ice cream from a passing vendor. She
unwraps it and holds it out to me. My defenses melt. After two
weeks of rigorous attention to all food and water that passed
my lips, I lick the sweet street fare, sacrificing my intestinal

health to this little girl's pleasure at hosting a visitor with all she could offer.

She's an only child who doesn't know her age. It was particularly ironic that we had first met outside the Al Mustanseria University, the world's oldest science college, built in 1233. This school-less girl's only education is learned navigating the streets outside the university's ancient walls.

I empty my purse of *dinars,* stuffing the oily bills into her plastic purse. She gleefully buys another ice cream for us to share.

Military helicopters zigzag overhead. Rumors that the American troops had closed bridges and jammed traffic make us jittery. Nebras escorts me out of the dicey *souk,* grabbing my hand and expertly keeping my skirt from being snagged by the ubiquitous wartime razor wire.

As we pass a store being repainted, she mentions it had been hit during the war's initial attacks. She had spent the long nights of the early bombings in a nearby mosque.

I hug her harder than I intended. I feel her wiry hair against my cheek, her grungy T-shirt against my shoulder, her warm, open heart so willing to accept mine.

And then I'm gone.

Shanti Elke Bannwart was born in Hamburg, Germany, at the onset of World War II. The experience of war during childhood formed her view on life. In 1982, after living in Switzerland and Scotland, she immigrated to the United States to study psychology. Today, Bannwart, in her seventies, lives in Santa Fe, New Mexico, and is a licensed counselor and life-coach, a spiritual seeker and elder, and is devoted to "Reflective Activism" on the issues of war and peace. (She is cofounder of Women for Peace and is a member of Women in Black.) She received an MFA in Creative Writing from Goddard College, and her essays have been published in national and international magazines, including *Pitkin Literary Magazine, The Santa Fe Sun, Aquila, Tokyo Advocate*, and she has been awarded prizes and finalist standing in several national contests. Her memoir, *Dancing on One Foot*, was published by Sunstone Press in 2012. In the following essay, the grandniece of Nazi Hermann Göring, Bettina Goering, seeks redemption by facing Holocaust survivor and artist Ruth Rich in Sidney, Australia. The documentary film of this journey, *Bloodlines*, has been shown during film festivals around the globe, including in Israel, and a second documentary is being negotiated between Bannwart and Moscow TV, whose producers want to explore this essay's message further.

Tightrope Across the Abyss

Shanti Elke Bannwart

Bettina lives on top of the mesa in a hand-built adobe house with turquoise-colored trim and window frames. The High Desert of New Mexico is her backyard. Bettina is my neighbor. "Neighborhood" at the outskirts of Santa Fe means distances of several miles between us. Bettina Goering has a slim face, blond hair, lively eyes, and a quick smile that lingers, comes and goes like shadows of the fast-moving clouds across this serene landscape. Her front teeth are just uneven enough to indicate that she might not have American roots. She does not; Bettina, like me, was born in Germany and is the descendent of Nazi ancestors. Her grandfather's brother was Hermann Göring. In case you are too young to recognize this name: Hermann Göring was the perfectly blond and Arian profiled German officer, the right-hand of Adolf Hitler; he was the Marshal of the Empire, the leader of the SS, founder of the feared GESTAPO and commander of the *Luftwaffe*. Hermann Göring concocted and condoned the concept of the concentration camps, where in perfectly engineered gas chambers and extermination ovens more than six million, mostly Jewish, human beings were destroyed.

I live at the foot of the mesa where Bettina has settled. New Mexico is about as far away as one can flee to separate from one's German roots and culture, but not far enough, I found out, to avoid meeting a compatriot who is the grandniece of Hermann Göring. For years I didn't know about her ancestral bondage and burden. We rarely met and simply said "Hello!" when we encountered each other along the dirt road. I didn't know that she was a Göring, even when her husband Adi functioned as an electrician and connected my 380-feet-deep well pump with the meter. Water is precious here in the High Desert and there are houses on top of the mesa that lack a well. A mesa is a flat table of land that is shaped and marked by canyons, valleys, and deep fissures. Our Rowe Mesa spreads for hundreds of miles and can be identified from a space shuttle.

I learn about Bettina's ancestry when a friend mentions during dinner, "Do you know that Bettina created a documentary about her pilgrimage to a Jewish artist in Australia who is a concentration camp survivor? Bettina's last name is Göring. She is the grandniece of Hitler's right-hand and officially designated successor."

This friend informs me where I would be able to buy the film, and so I do. It stands waiting for months between books on my shelf, before I gather the courage to view it. I am German, too, was born at the onset of World War II, and my soul and identity is scarred by this history. I still feel unable to talk about the Holocaust without weeping, more than sixty years after the events. I am perpetrator by lineage and cultural inheritance.

I finally gather my courage and view the documentary; it moves me deeply. The images sink into layers of the past where they merge with memories of my own German history. My father was a Nazi, decorated by Hitler with the Iron Cross of Merit. I feel less alone and branded when I discover that Bettina, too, suffers the phenomenon of grief and guilt by association with her German origin.

One day, when driving to Santa Fe along the dirt road that leads out of the canyon, I slow down at the cattle guard. Another car comes my way and stops. Our windows are aligned, and when I open mine, Bettina is looking at me. With one glance, and for the first time, we recognize each other as sisters of fate.

"Shanti," she says, "I heard that you bought my video."

"Bettina," I respond, "I want to meet and talk with you."

Again, I postpone, for months, connecting with her. I am afraid, shy, terrified, like one would be before open-heart surgery. I fear to be found out, to be discovered with a black sore inside that has been there for most of my life and will remain until the end. I dread the anguish that radiates from that spot—it cannot be soothed. Weeks later, Bettina invites me to a public viewing of the film in the small and intimate Jean Cocteau Theater in Santa Fe. A painful discussion follows the performance.

And this is the story that the documentary portrays: Made aware by a friend, Bettina discovers the art of the Australian painter Ruth Rich, who creates pictures of concentration camps and their victims; it is dark, brooding, heart-wrenching art. Her images burrow into the subconscious rivers of horror that flow underneath the physical reality of those camps. Ruth is a renowned artist and has shown her work in two major exhibitions in Australia. Bettina Goering studies the artwork on Ruth's website and begins an email correspondence with the artist. This emerging relationship encourages Bettina to attempt the healing of her own ancestral wounding, of her guilt and shame, by meeting face to face with this survivor, whose loved ones were gassed during the Nazi regime.

"Oh my god," Bettina sighs and distorts her face, "it's going to be work."

The camera follows her on this journey to Australia and documents with touching simplicity a thoroughly womanly approach to atonement: being there, eye to eye with the "Enemy." The fright before meeting the guest shows in Ruth Rich's face as she stands at the Sidney airport, waiting to encounter Bettina.

"I am totally overwhelmed," she says in tears, squeezing the wilting sunflowers in her hands.

The two women meet as strangers, drink tea, circle, and test each other as they begin to talk. It is hot in Australia. They sweat and get tired, anxious, and nervous as well as intimate in their revelations. The physicality of these encounters is stunning, perplexing, and heart-wrenching. Bettina and Ruth search inside themselves for the courage to be torn open and made vulnerable. They struggle to come to terms with a horrific historical event by scaling it down to a personal encounter. They demonstrate politics of the heart and soul, a female approach to making peace through personal action and down-to-earth, awkward meetings and exposure.

"Are you willing to be uncomfortable with me?" asks Ruth.

"To have courage and make myself vulnerable, I need physical contact," says Bettina. They stretch their hands toward each other and hold on.

"We need to step into the water together," says Ruth.

Making peace is hard work, like giving birth. It is painful, humbling, and sometimes very ordinary and sweaty. A big universal story is encapsulated in this small encounter. Horror is transformed into forgiveness through the physical closeness of two deeply wounded human beings. The surface of this meeting seems gentle and sometimes tentative and polite, but underneath flows a bloody river. This is Herculean work, enacted humbly in a small house in Bangalow, Australia.

"A lot of Jewish survivors would not agree with me, meeting a Nazi descendent," mentions Ruth, as if she is surprised by her own generosity.

"I understand," says Bettina. "I feel total outrage about our inheritance. At thirty I got sterilized. I didn't want to give birth to more monsters; I cut my bloodline. A radical decision. My brother did the same, independently. I had three mental breakdowns and could not sleep for weeks."

After many days of confrontation and healing, Bettina Goering and Ruth Rich desire to perform a final ritual that will bring closure to their journey. They apply to celebrate a peace ceremony in the Jewish Museum in Sidney. Their request is declined. But the World Peace Organization steps into the breach, staging a peace rite with candles, tears, embraces. During this celebration of forgiveness, these two women stand in for millions.

"This was my life work, to get this over with," sighs Bettina, exhausted.

"We have become friends," says Ruth.

This encounter portrays a glorious and practical example of the path toward reconciliation and change. This is not the way official politics is practiced, but it seems more effective and engaging than formal talks. Intimately videotaped by Cynthia Connop, the documentary *Bloodlines* is slowly finding its path around the world, being shown and discussed at the Boston Jewish Film Festival and at the Jewish Film Festivals in Israel, in October 2008, when Bettina was invited to travel to Jerusalem and attend the presentation.

A two-page reportage appears in the *HAARETZ* – Israeli News source, with the title: "Goering's Grandniece Seeks Closure in Israel." The online report triggers more than forty responses from readers. Here are just a few excerpts:

· This woman has been hounded beyond sanity. Does she really think her own seed is evil? What a bizarre, Medieval notion. What a grotesque story. What a grotesque world.

· Hermann Goering was a Nazi and committed crimes that are simply unforgivable but it is a problem for him only, not for his family. Nobody can be kept guilty for crimes committed by parents or relatives.

· Any Jew who cannot feel empathy for this woman does not understand the essence of being Jewish.

Weeks later, Bettina visits my home and we have tea.

"I need to learn to forgive my own people," she says. "I have a lot of compassion for the Germans and their history. My father adored his uncle, Hermann Göring, and I feel shame that I liked him when I was a child."

"Your honesty helps me to come out of the closet," I admit. "Now I can talk more freely about my past. I am softening around it, as if ice is melting inside me."

I have not yet forgiven my people; it's a burden I carry. I hope that this confrontation might become a catalyst for my own growth. But now, after reading the responses to Bettina's appearance in Israel, I feel relieved, free, almost joyous. Yes, maybe we both can let go and shake the old shadows off. Maybe we are not responsible, not guilty and tainted by our ancestry.

"Bettina," I say, "your journey into reconciliation broke a spell. Your courage to face the victim and accuser took the rocks out of the river of my conscience and allows the water to flow. The reactions of the Jewish people to your video reveal that the children of the Holocaust victims encourage movement towards a new story."

"Maybe it is time for the next generation after the Nazis to kick the demons out and invest our energy, compassion, and love into our own present lives and into the country, where we live now."

We hug and I have the sense that a rusty lock in my chest is cracking open.

As I write this, I sit in the small library room of the Anasazi Hotel in Santa Fe. A fire crackles in the fireplace. On the mantel stands a carved wooden angel wielding a sword in one hand and the scale of justice in the other. The beautiful face is fierce and serene. She looks as if she knows how to use this sword and will not hesitate to apply force for a worthy cause. Does she discern, because she is an angel, when drawing blood is justified?

I come here from time to time, reading, writing, and musing and enjoying the art of the three cultures that live peacefully together in New Mexico. In this room, the Hispanic influence is represented by the carved angel in its simple beauty, the Native American by the exquisite ceramic pots and baskets displayed on the shelves, and the Anglo by the blond lady in front of this room who handles requests for trips, tickets, and rental cars with the help of her laptop. Friendly tourism seems to benefit all three cultures. It took some hundreds of years to find this arrangement among races with such contrary philosophies. I think it's the work of people in their ordinary lives that weaves the bonds between cultures. Here, too, the intricate games of politics are less powerful than people's respectful human interactions.

It's all layered together and exists in close proximity: normal everyday activities and joys exist side by side with the big events that shake and destroy cultures. The same people who guard concentration camps sit at the dinner table with their families and laugh.

"How can a normal citizen turn into a mass murderer without realizing it?" asks Bettina in the documentary. Yes, how is it possible that light and darkness can be so interconnected and "not know about each other?" Bettina is a doctor and healer, and she is also the grandniece of a mass murderer and fears that she might carry his homicidal genes. Hermann Göring was an insane criminal, and he was also a likable man, jovial, admired by the people. He had style and believed himself to be a hero, assured that his fame would spread across the world. When he was accused and put on trial in Nuremberg, he still argued that his deeds were justified. Deemed guilty and ordered to be hanged, he poisoned himself two hours before his execution.

I live between the last fingers of the Sangre de Christo Mountains, in the High Desert of extreme beauty and harshness; but only ten miles from my home hides one of the most important battlefields of the bloody American Civil War: Glorieta Pass, where in 1862 the Union forces stopped the Confederates from expanding into the West, toward the Pacific Ocean.

It seems that civilization is a very thin net underneath the tightrope that spans the abyss of our dark passions and cruelties. We had better tread gently, keeping a careful and humble balance so that we don't slip.

Two women dared to dance on this rope. And didn't fall.

THE TRAGEDY OF THE COLOR LINE

"Herein lies the tragedy of the age: . . . that men know so little of men."

— W. E. B. Du Bois (1868–1963), *The Souls of Black Folk*, 1903

A Dash of Pepper in the Snow Samuel Autman

"Miss Otis Regrets" Mary Elizabeth Parker

Signatures Lyzette Wanzer

Growing up in an all-black neighborhood in St. Louis, Missouri, **Samuel Autman**'s most striking intercultural exposure occurred when he was in high school. Curious about the environment and ecology, he enrolled in an outdoor education and leadership program at the Missouri Botanical Garden. In that program, he met black, white, and Asian students from other parts of the city and the suburbs. What struck him most were the varieties of religious backgrounds and traditions many of these students hailed from, including Buddhism, Christian Science, Judaism, and Quakerism, to name a few. Later, in the early 1990s, Autman became the first black reporter for the *Salt Lake Tribune* in Utah ("A Dash of Pepper in the Snow" details this experience). He received his MFA in narrative nonfiction from Columbia University in 2008, and his essays have been published online in such journals as *Brevity* and in the recent anthology *Resilience*, edited by Eric Nguyen. He has also received honorable mentions from several contests including the University of New Orleans Study Abroad nonfiction contest. Currently, as the only black creative writing professor at DePauw University, Indiana, he's drawn to writings highlighting people who are outsiders due to race, gender, spirituality, sexuality, or class.

A Dash of Pepper in the Snow

Samuel Autman

The first time I caught a glimpse of Salt Lake City, Utah, was from an airplane window at an altitude of about 10,000 feet in October 1992. From that vantage point the Great Salt Lake looked like a dead, muddy tributary of the Mississippi River, cradled in a desolate terrain, much like a NASA picture from the surface of Mars. Air pockets over the mountains created a bumpy descent into Salt Lake City International Airport. I felt uneasy. The pilot's words over the intercom didn't soothe. I worried that the plane might crash. But we landed safely. Disembarking, I squinted at the sunshine. The Utah skies contained brightness not present in Oklahoma or Missouri. The open space, crisp air, and snow-covered slopes testified that I had stepped into a part of the American landscape of which I knew little—a real, live post card.

The airport was much larger than Tulsa's. I was in town for the weekend to interview for a reporting job at the *Salt Lake*

Tribune, something I had concealed from my editors at the *Tulsa World* where I was the obituary writer. Ultimately I craved a cushy gig at a big metropolitan daily like the *Los Angeles Times*, the *New York Times*, or the *Washington Post*, but the pathway to a bigger newspaper meant bouncing from city to city. Walking through the airport, I was struck by the number of children running around and playing with one another; many with brilliant blond hair, many who had obviously been spending lots of time in the sun. Even at the *World* I was the only black writer on the staff, so being the only black person in the room, the airplane, or for as far as the eye could see didn't bother me. Or so I thought.

A few months later I accepted the staff writing position, unknowingly becoming the first black reporter ever hired at the *Tribune*. No one realized this fact, not even the paper itself. (Sometimes history is made during routine events, like when taking a job.) In my first week in January 1993, three colleagues invited me to lunch at a favorite *Tribune* hangout, Lamb's Grill Café, a restaurant owned by Greeks and established in 1919. The interior didn't appear to have changed much since Woodrow Wilson left office. The walls were dark wood and held pictures of presidents George Washington and Abraham Lincoln. The carpet was a deep antebellum red, the tables covered with flowers and ironed white linens.

We chatted and ordered our drinks from the waitress, who wore a traditional uniform with a nametag, "Val," on her lapel. Her blond hair was pulled up with a pin, and she looked to be in her early forties. Think Flo from the former CBS show *Alice*, the loud-talking one who always told people to "Kiss my grits." From the looks of her weathered hands, Val had seen some hard days. The place bustled at noontime, the room reverberating with conversations, a cacophony of voices. Lamb's was a place where Utah's movers and shakers lunched, mostly white men in white shirts, mostly lawyers, businessmen, politicians. I was the only black person in the establishment. My new colleagues were talking about local politics when Val slid our iced teas and sodas before us.

Soon, she arrived back with our food and gave me a stern look. "Sir, could you move that saucer out of the way so I can sit your clam chowder down?"

"Yes, ma'am," I said, nodding.

"Thank you, sir. That's mighty white of you," she snapped.

The idle chatter at our table ceased as Val set everyone's food down. An uncomfortable awkwardness gripped us for a moment. Eyes darted around the table to register facial expressions. Val left.

"What the f—— was that about?" one person asked.

"Did you hear what she said to him?" asked another.

"I don't know what her problem is. Let's eat," I said.

I pretended her comment didn't rub me the wrong way. It had. Maybe it was just an innocent one, I reasoned. But the silence and discomfort lingered over our table when Val came back. Later, when we left the restaurant and walked back into the newspaper building, my colleagues expressed bewilderment. Back when I was an undergraduate in the mid-1980s in a small town in southeast Missouri, I had heard someone call me the N-word from another room. So I was versed in any number of cutting racial remarks. "Mighty white of you" was not among them.

The Val incident initiated me into a three-and-a-half-year era of such interactions with many waitresses and service industry workers. Fidgety sales clerks eyeballed me as I walked down every aisle in certain department stores. One man at a 7-Eleven in Provo called the police because "there's a black guy in here." It was the most vexing of times. Many times I wondered, Is this person staring because I am six-foot-four, black, or both? These are the unseen mental jumping jacks many people of color navigate when they live in cities and small towns where the citizens don't often have faces like their own.

And this was just the beginning.

Reporters don't keep secrets. Stories of the restaurant incident spread through the newsroom. Within minutes Jay Shelledy, the editor who had hired me, caught whiff of the Val story. During my job interview back in the fall, before I joined the staff, he asserted that racial encounters would not likely be a factor for me in Utah. Utahans were not exposed to many black people; they weren't hateful, he had said. Now I was being summoned into Shelledy's office so he could hear my version of the event. I took a seat.

Shelledy was in his fifties. He had a long face and a large midsection. Shelledy's hair was light brown and the expression on his face was more of an upside-down smile than a scowl.

When he spoke it sounded like he wasn't completely opening his mouth, like he had a few marbles rolling around, but that didn't stop him from barking at people with the certainty that let us all know he was the guy in charge.

"What happened down there, Autman?"

I told the story. He listened with empathy that quickly gurgled into anger. "That's completely unacceptable. I'm gonna take care of this," he said.

Before too long, he was on the telephone to restaurant owner Jake Agnew. I couldn't hear the conversation, but I saw Shelledy and Travel Editor Tom McCarthey, whose family owned the newspaper, bolt out of the building in their suits and ties. About 20 minutes later Shelledy came over to my desk and said that Agnew wanted to speak to me in the hall. I hadn't done anything, but I felt singled out. The last thing I wanted to evoke was sympathy for being black, but Agnew was on the other side of the door, waiting. I quietly got up from my desk, the child in trouble.

Agnew was a middle-aged man who wore glasses and had his gray hair pulled back into a ponytail. He wore a shirt and tie and a nice pair of slacks. I extended my hand.

"Young man, I am really very sorry. Her name is Val. She doesn't even remember saying it. I'll fire her if you want me to," he said.

"Don't worry about it. I don't want her to get fired. I just want you to know that it is uncomfortable to have to hear a comment like that over lunch."

"I understand and I promise you, it won't happen again."

He placed a $25 gift certificate in my hand. I recoiled. Why would I go back there? Even if Val didn't mean to say anything racist, she would remember me now and might spit a big wad in my soup the next time. I swallowed my resistance, shook his hand, and accepted the certificate. He looked relieved, making me promise to return to his establishment. I agreed, promising myself I wouldn't.

Shelledy had assured me many things when I had interviewed for the job in Salt Lake City: I shouldn't expect racist remarks; it didn't snow much in Utah—at least it hadn't in his few years there. Sure, it snowed a lot in the mountains and at the ski resorts like Deer Valley and Snowbird, but the white stuff didn't cover the Salt Lake Valley, where most people lived.

A few weeks after I arrived, Utah lived up to the phrase printed on the state's license plates—"The Greatest Snow on Earth"—when a snowstorm dumped 42 inches in the valley, shutting the government down for several days. At more than 3 feet, the snow was up to my belly button. The schools closed. The streets were snarled because the snowplows couldn't keep up. Even some intrepid *Tribune* reporters couldn't leave their driveways. It was a beautiful, white terror—snow hell.

Salt Lake City is a stunning place, especially in snowdrifts. Encased by the Wasatch Mountain range, it's hard to find a place in the city that doesn't have a splendid view of the mountains. They soothe and reassure. The streets are always clean, with little or no trash anywhere, so different from St. Louis, where I grew up. What most people notice immediately about Salt Lake City is the width of the streets. Folklore tells that Brigham Young wanted to be able to lock arms with all twenty-seven of his wives and turn around in the streets with them. A more likely but apocryphal explanation is that he wanted to be able to turn around in the streets while driving his horse and buggy.

One night after work, I pulled my Toyota into the parking lot of Mac Frugal's, a big discount store on 400 Street South and 500 Street East. That would be four blocks south and five blocks east of the Temple, the worldwide headquarters of the Church of Jesus Christ of Latter-day Saints (LDS), and ground zero in downtown Salt Lake City. The blocks are all configured by their relationship to the Temple.

The wind was bitingly cold. In the parking lot a woman with a little boy was fidgeting with the car door, having inadvertently locked the keys in her vehicle. When I walked by, the little boy stood shivering as his mother tried to break into her own car, no doubt to get home. I paused for a moment, watching her struggle, her frustration obvious.

"Excuse me, sir, could you help me?" the woman asked.

"Uh, I don't know what I can do. You want me to try to help you with my jumper cables or something?" I asked.

"No, but you know how to do this, don't you?"

"Know how to do what?"

"Break in. You know how to break into cars, don't you?" The words rolled easily off her lips.

The wind was exceedingly cold and the little boy shivered

more and wanted to get home. More for the child than for her, I went over and tried to help pry the door open. I didn't know how to break into cars any more than I knew how to rap or shoot a basketball. Or a bullet. After several tries with a coat hanger, I turned to her and said, "Sorry, ma'am, I can't get it," and strode into the store. I left them standing in the cold.

All the reporters at the *Tribune* covering news for the city desk rotated to cover weekend shifts. As the new guy, I had my share of Saturday and Sunday assignments, covering everything from parades, to political announcements from merchants angling to make it into the Sunday paper, the day that captured the most readers. The event that day was a public speech.

The speaker was a redhead with tiny glasses and a short, neat haircut. She told roughly one hundred junior and senior high school–age girls attending a math and science conference at the University of Utah that they should not let any obstacle block them from pursuing any field of study, especially the sciences. One of her professors at the Mormon Church–owned Brigham Young University, the nation's biggest private university, told her when she earned a mediocre grade in his chemistry class: "You should have stopped when you had the chance." She had taken his challenge and went on to study medicine. The girls cheered. She advised them that if they would excel in math and science, they would find many career opportunities. The girls and their mothers cheered.

I took notes during the speech, using Gregg Shorthand, which I had learned in high school because I never liked going back to listen to tape recorders. After her speech I wandered around the room talking to what the *Tribune* editor called "RPs," or "Real People," which in this case included young girls and their mothers, about their impressions of the speaker. A university employee suddenly tapped me on the shoulder.

"You can start breaking these tables and chairs down now. This event is over," she said.

"Excuse me?"

"Aren't you on the maintenance staff?" She glanced at the casual clothes I wore when reporting. "You can start breaking these tables and chairs down," she said.

"Uh, no, I am not. I am here from the *Salt Lake Tribune*, writing a story on the speaker."

"Ohhh. I'm so sorry. I thought you were from the maintenance crew," she said, laughing nervously to hide her embarrassment.

I sighed, smirked, rolled my eyes, and walked away.

In the early 1990s, the U.S. Census Bureau reported that 94 percent of the people who lived in Utah were white. The remaining 6 percent was composed of mostly Latinos who lived in West Valley City, a large suburb west of Salt Lake City, along with Native Americans who had reservations scattered through the edge of the state, and Asians and Pacific Islanders, mostly Tongans and Samoans, some of whom had been brought to Utah via conversions to Mormonism. Less than 1 percent of the state's residents were black. I'd known the black population would be sparse, but it never occurred to me there would be so few that I'd want to run up and hug every black person I saw, a result of being the first black reporter to ever work at the *Tribune* in its 122-year history.

My colleagues at the paper were mostly liberal Mormons, or "jack Mormons," which means they were born into an LDS family but had drifted from the faith. Unlike devout Mormons, some drank coffee or even harder stuff.

These liberal Mormons were incredibly friendly, for the most part people politically to the left who joined me for beer from time to time at a place called D.B. Coopers, another hangout. I felt welcomed by the staff, and years after I'd left Utah, I went back and stayed in the homes of people I'd befriended in those days. For the most part, the newspaper was a safe ship where I was insulated from racially insensitive remarks. Shelledy would not tolerate such comments from his staff. But beyond the sphere of the newspaper, I had to navigate a world where Utah Jazz player Karl Malone was a hero, but even he, too, had complained of the awkwardness of it all. I couldn't dissect whether Mormonism bred ignorant racist comments or whether they were simply bred by the absence of black people in the church and state.

On a Sunday in May 1993, I was sent out to the Salt Lake City Holiday Inn at the airport to cover a convention of psychics. I didn't really believe in psychics but these weekend assignments broke up the monotony of covering school board meetings, which had become my routine assignment by then.

Much of journalism is making certain that the talking heads are speaking the truth, which requires some of the reporter's own discoveries, so I wandered around the convention halls talking to various men and women at their tables. Someone introduced me to the fair's coordinator, a short, older woman with blond hair mixed with gray. Her glasses and diminutive stature made her look like a typical Utah grandmother immersed in psychic phenomena as an art form. She had been a psychic for decades and then operated her own fortune-telling business in Sugarhouse, a popular Salt Lake City neighborhood. We made small talk, and then she proceeded to compliment me.

"You're such an educated colored," she said.

The word did jumping jacks in my ears. "Excuse me?"

"You're an educated colored. Most of the coloreds we Utahans are used to seeing are lowlifes," she said.

I didn't react, but after months of rude stares, zealous clerks at stores, I was exploding inside. A quiet rage erupted into a newspaper column about my experiences as a black man in Utah for the first six months.

I had grown up in highly segregated St. Louis, where generally the blacks lived in the north part of the city and county. The few white city dwellers resided on the south side; most lived in the western suburbs. In the city's Central West End, the artists, social progressives, upper-income people, and gay people mixed in this neutral ground. Over time, because of my interests and where I could find jobs, my world became whiter and whiter, be it in journalism school in Columbia, Missouri, or as the only black writer on staff at the *Tulsa World* from 1989 to 1992 in a county with a 13 percent black population. Now my job was in Salt Lake, perhaps one of the whitest areas in the world.

On May 30, 1993, my column appeared:

> I swore I would never write a commentary piece on racism in Utah. But a psychic's remark pushed me over the threshold of public timidity. Last Sunday I was assigned to cover a psychic fair at a Salt Lake City Holiday Inn. Only a crystal ball could have prepared me for what was coming.
>
> While interviewing the fair coordinator, a Salt Lake City–based psychic, I was spinning my wheels, seeking an angle on an unusual story. This woman, who operates out

of Sugar House, described her metaphysical art form. She spoke of her ongoing client list. She had been fortune-telling for decades.

During the interview she said, "You are an educated colored. Most of the coloreds we Utahans are used to seeing are lowlifes."

Colored? Who uses such outdated vernacular? I sat in amazement. Her razor-sharp words left wounds. She might as well have slapped me. That might have been less painful.

Since my January relocation from Tulsa, Okla., to Salt Lake City, I have been inundated with racist remarks, rude stares and unfriendly vibes. Zealous sales clerks, who never let me out of their sight, are the worst. After hearing "Is there anything I can help you with?" four times in 15 minutes, I am ready to scream: "My Creator endowed me with a mouth. When I seek help, I will ask for it!"

The column related the incident about Val and continued:

Who hasn't seen those greyhounds and fire hoses turned on that poor woman in Birmingham, Ala.? I interned at the *Birmingham Post–Herald* during the summer of 1988. I experienced no verbal abuse there. Maybe those television clips of the fire hoses and greyhounds embarrassed Birmingham so much they made a collective decision to overcome those images.

It is somewhat unfair to compare Birmingham in 1988 to Salt Lake City in 1993, but they serve as my reference points. Could it be that Birmingham of the late 1980s is more advanced in social relations than Salt Lake City of the early 1990s?

After relating several more incidents from my repertoire, I closed with:

"Utah! You are moving to Utah? I hope you know what you are doing." This chorus friends and families sang to me daily before I moved here. I relocated against warnings. I visited before making the decision.

It seemed like a good idea and I love the *Tribune*. But as

a black man in Utah, my struggle controls me.

As I look into my crystal ball, I see Utah becoming more diverse, and the inevitable question comes to mind: "Will Utahans become sensitive to people of color or will they remain socially in the dinosaur age?"

The column hit the city like a bomb. I was simultaneously rattled by all the responses and yet relieved to be able to dump this problem into the newspaper. Letters and phone calls poured in, mostly supportive, a few critical. A local AM radio program had me on live, enduring a few hostile calls. Most people's letters to the editor were supportive, but there was an undercurrent of, "If you don't like it, get your ass out." The following week, I got a phone call from the psychic.

"Why did you write that?" she said angrily over the telephone. "I'm not a racist."

"Well, ma'am, I didn't say you were a racist," I said, keeping my cool. "I said you made a racist remark."

"You need to correct that. I'm not a racist. I got calls from a bunch of people I know." She went on to say that she had a close relative who was married to a black man, and with that fact, how could she be a racist?

I didn't apologize. Neither did the paper run a correction or a retraction. There was nothing to correct.

Months later, the *Tribune* editors sent me out to do a back-to-school story at a house in Taylorsville, a suburb west of Salt Lake City. The family was months away from having three times the number of children as were in that popular seventies television show—*The Brady Bunch*. My assignment: When there are seventeen kids in the house, what does it take for mom and dad to get everyone ready to go to school? Like any other day in Utah, I had no idea on earth what to expect.

They lived in a blue two-story house with six bedrooms adjacent to Interstate 215. The first person I remember seeing was Martha, the mother. Holding a baby in one arm, she extended her hand to greet me. Wearing glasses, and encircled by six smaller children, she was stout and wore a plain dress and a permanent smile on her face. A genuinely friendly woman, she showed me around their property. Tiny eyes peeked around the corner, curious to see the tall, strange black man who had come into their home. The half-acre backyard was quite a playground, with a trampoline, sand lot, six bicycles, and a swing set.

Getting them ready for school was a Herculean task, almost the stuff of children's fairy tales. The children, all seventeen of them, represented every grade except first and tenth. She told me they arose in three shifts daily to prepare for school: 5:30, 6:30, and 7 a.m. All of the children older than ten had to shower, iron their clothing, and fix their own breakfasts. Once they finished their chores, they had to help their younger siblings do the same.

The military structure came from Hal, their father, a twenty-six-year veteran of the U.S. Marine Corps. "There's nothing in this world that works without a plan," he said. "They teach you that in boot camp." He seemed like her perfect match, also husky but a bit gruffer. His was clearly the hand of discipline in that family.

The couple and I sat in the living room to talk more about what it took to get so many kids ready for school on a daily basis. Martha told me that in previous years she was getting up before the children and making ten lunches daily, requiring a gallon of milk, a loaf of bread, and a pile of bologna. They'd since decided it was easier to buy all their lunches at school instead.

I couldn't help but ask, Why had they so many children?

Almost as if on script, Martha spoke up. "I love being pregnant," she said, patting her stomach, indicating that number eighteen was on the way. "I have known since I was a little girl I would have a big family. I thought it would be ten or twelve. I had no idea it would be seventeen."

Hal said they were practicing Mormons and their philosophy on procreation was in part derived from the belief that millions of souls are in heaven waiting for earthly parents to bring them into the earth. He looked me in the eye and said, "All of those little spirits need a place to come. We'd rather have them come to our house than be born on the streets of Rio de Janeiro or south central Los Angeles."

In other words, good white Utah families, not families of color. Had I been a white reporter the comment might not have registered as racially insensitive. Of course had I been white, he probably wouldn't have felt the need to say it. But as a black man living in Utah, I found myself wondering what these people meant. I was getting angrier by the day, living in Utah, and eventually became seized by a desire to leave.

Many months later I was living in a neighborhood called The Avenues, considered progressive and hip, when someone knocked on the front door. Ted, the roommate I had taken, was a college student who brewed beer in our tiny kitchen and watched endless episodes of MTV's *Beavis and Butthead*. Most of all he was a Mormon mocker. He loved inviting missionaries over to taunt them. Feigning interest in their faith, he leaned forward and listened to their spiel. When they asked if he believed in Jesus Christ, he said, "Yeah, I believe in Jesus, but what was he on?" Jeff had no intention of converting to Mormonism.

There they stood, two attractive, college-age women with literature in hand. They identified themselves as missionaries from the Church of Jesus Christ of Latter-day Saints.

"May we have a few minutes of your time, Brother Sam?" asked Sister Thurman, a blond woman with shoulder-length hair and glasses, squeezing her *Book of Mormon*.

Sister Thurman had unwittingly put her finger on something in calling me Brother Sam. I had been a lifelong seeker of spiritual Truth, having sampled from a smorgasbord of philosophies including Baptist, Buddhist, and Pentecostal. I had moved to Salt Lake City to shed my charismatic Christian identity and to start life anew. I understood and appreciated a missionary's zeal to preach and convert, but she had knocked on the wrong door. The real reason I let them in was to answer my questions about Mormonism.

They had outlined the tenets of their faith for about 15 minutes when I sighed. Sister Thurman was using note cards.

"Can you quit looking down at that and speak to me from what's in your own heart?"

"Excuse me?" she asked.

"Don't you know what you believe without having to read that script?"

She was quiet for a second and then asked, "What would you like to know about our church?"

"What I really want to know is why I would join a philosophy that says I am cursed because of the color of my skin."

She thought about it for a second. "Well, it says in the Book of Mormon that the Lord did darken both the heart and skin of the wicked."

"Precisely. So why would I, a black man, join that?" My voice rose. "What makes you think I would want to be in the LDS church? What does it hold for me?"

"Well, I can see that you have an argumentative spirit, which is really a demon. We're going to have to leave," she said.

My horns grew. The demons in me, combined with my wicked black skin, were ready for a scriptural rumble. "You still haven't answered my question. What was your name again? Sister Thurman?"

They closed their Books of Mormon and Doctrines and Covenants and scrambled to get out of my apartment, telling me they would pray for my immortal soul. I thanked them for coming by and wished them well. That wasn't my only encounter with the faithful about this subject. Those missionaries had exposed what I had heard all along, that the Mormon Church had racism not only embedded in its philosophy but its sacred texts as well.

I am loathe to lay all the blame for my Utah experiences at the feet of the Mormon Church or the Mormons, but it would be derelict to ignore practices or doctrines of the LDS church that might have contributed to racism. Numerous passages in the Book of Mormon refer to the wicked dark people, none more egregious than 2 Nephi 5:21:

And he had caused the cursing to come upon them, yea, even a sore cursing, because of their iniquity. For behold, they had hardened their hearts against him, that they had become like unto a flint; wherefore, as they were white, and exceedingly fair and delightsome, that they might not be enticing unto my people the Lord God did cause a skin of blackness to come upon them.

It's hard to interpret this passage as meaning anything but whiteness is goodness and darkness is evil. I was over the moon to learn that the phrase "skin of blackness" from this very passage was removed from the online Book of Mormon in late 2010. It's an important baby step. Much more is needed.

Other verses expressly forbid the faithful to marry the cursed dark ones. Black men could not, as a result, hold the priesthood in the Mormon Church. The church was excoriated over this and did a lot of fancy dancing. As the times changed, so did the position on black males as priests. In a surprising move, President Spenser Kimball in 1978 announced that he had received a revelation that black men could hold the priesthood, reversing years of institutional racism. Seems like the time calls for even bolder moves.

I've gone back to Utah many times since leaving in 1996, for the Sundance Film Festival and to visit friends. Each time there are more black people walking through the streets of downtown Salt Lake City. They tell me people continue to stare but I get the impression a change has come to Utah. Mormons are quick to point to Gladys Knight as an example of a black Mormon. Knight, who converted to Mormonism in 1998, won a Grammy in 2006 for a gospel recording called *One Voice* by Gladys Knight and the Saints Unified Voices. Utah and Mormonism continue to make national news, everything from the 2002 Winter Olympics to HBO's *Big Love*, Elizabeth Smart's kidnapping case, the Republican candidate for the U.S. presidency (Mitt Romney), and the church's financial support to defeat Proposition 8, the gay marriage amendment in California; Americans have an insatiable fascination for all things Mormon.

But then the church would also do admirable things behind the scenes that few people know about. In the mid-1980s, the Aryan Nation out of Idaho decided that Salt Lake City would be a perfect place to establish a chapter. To do so it had started a hate-spewing campaign. Planning to launch a radio station, it released hate-filled fliers at black churches. One day Rev. France Davis, the pastor of Calvary Baptist Church, the largest black church in the state, found copies of an "Open letter to various n——s" plastered on the church property. In vitriolic language, the writer wished blacks would go back to Africa, get AIDS, and, "better yet, haul them out to the garbage dump, pour gas on them and burn them." The letter was signed, "The KKK is active, alive and well. 5,000 strong in Utah."

Shortly after that, Davis skipped sitting in his pastoral study to run some errands. The next day he came to find bullet holes where he would have been studying.

"It was the Mormon Church who helped us run those people out of here," he said years later. "They organized a campaign, kept them off the radio, and kept the Aryan Nation out of Salt Lake City. They have proven to be good citizens."

Eventually I was offered a reporting position at the *St. Louis Post–Dispatch* in August 1996, emancipating myself from three-and-a-half years of dizzying encounters. Jay Shelledy and I pulled out my $25 certificate from Lamb's Grill Café and went back right before I left. We laughed and talked about the old incident. He told me I had been a good, productive reporter and if I ever wanted to come back and work for him, I always had a job waiting for me in Salt Lake City. I didn't see Val at the restaurant that day.

Strangely, my friends from that era, all white, had bonded with me as non-Mormons navigating a valley that was thirty years behind the rest of the nation socially. Over time, I have been able to regale people at cocktail parties with my Salt Lake City anecdotes, leaving them stunned. But I kept going back to Salt Lake; I couldn't stay away. In fact, the further I got away from it, the more charming the wide and clean streets became, the more I missed my friends at the newspaper. In Utah I learned how to bond with people despite differences in religion and background. Whenever I go, there are any number of people who will pick me up at the airport and offer me their homes. Outside of my extended family in rural Arkansas, there's no place else on Earth where I have these kinds of bonds.

In the summer of 2006, ten years after I had left Utah and thirteen years after my encounter with Val at Lamb's Grill Café, I was in Salt Lake City doing some research. I wandered back into Lamb's. Main Street was just about boarded up. The *Tribune* had been sold and moved several blocks west of what had been a thriving artery to downtown. The Mormon Church had bought much of Main Street, which they planned to develop into a sort of Mormon Disney-like shopping complex, the details kept under wraps.

I walked into Lamb's and got a little nervous and nostalgic. I took copious notes on the interior of the place; it looked just as it did when I was there for the first time. I drank coffee and ate a donut. The waitress was friendly.

"Did you ever know a Val who worked here?"

"Just a second, sweetie. Does anybody remember a Val used to work here?" she yelled into a back room. They had heard of her but she was long gone.

As I was about to leave I noticed Jake Agnew behind the cash register. I extended my hand, and asked if he remembered me. He paused. "You're the guy who had that episode with Val. Of course I remember you." We exchanged brief pleasantries and recalled that day's drama.

"You know the strange thing about that whole incident was that Val had been married to a black man. So I could never figure out why she said that to you."

"She *what?*"

"She had been married to a black man by the time you were here, was divorced. That's why it confounded us all so."

For years I had been telling people how this rude, nasty-mouthed woman had called me "mighty white." Sometime later, I learned it was an expression used by Eddie Murphy on NBC's *Saturday Night Live*. And although I didn't know exactly what she meant at the time (the *Urban Dictionary* says the phrase refers to "a charitable deed"), it didn't feel good. Now, everything I had thought about Val melted away. So the woman who had come to symbolize initiating me into Utah's racially insensitive culture had been married to a black man?

Maybe, just maybe, I had reminded Val of her ex-husband.

Mary Elizabeth Parker, a longtime transplant from Michigan to the South, is not a cultural adventurer except in that (minor) migration and in her marriage to (and subsequent travels with) her husband, a Jew born in Cairo of Italian ancestry and educated in British schools, who speaks Arabic, Hebrew, French, Italian, and English. Centuries before his family had migrated to Italy and then Cairo, following the textiles trade, his Sephardic ancestors had been expelled from Spain by King Ferdinand and Queen Isabella. Eventually they were also expelled from Egypt by President Nasser because they weren't Arabs. Her ancestors, Wesleyan Methodists propelled to America by poverty rather than political/religious persecution, were from Cornwall and Scotland. Parker's poetry collections include *The Sex Girl* (1999) and two chapbooks, *Breathing in a Foreign Country* (1993) and *That Stumbling Ritual* (1980). Her poems have appeared in many journals, including *Notre Dame Review, Gettysburg Review, New Letters, Arts & Letters, Confrontation,* and *Greensboro Review*; and in *Earth and Soul* (2001), an anthology published in English and Russian in the Kostroma region of Russia. She holds a PhD in Modern American and British Literature, was twice nominated for a Pushcart Prize, and is creator and chair of the Dana Awards.

"Miss Otis Regrets"

Mary Elizabeth Parker

> *When the mob came and got her / and dragged her from the jail, Madam, / they strung her from / the old willow 'cross the way / and the moment before she died, / she lifted up her lovely head and cried, "Madam. / Miss Otis regrets she's unable to lunch today."*
> — from **Ella Fitzgerald Sings the Cole Porter Song Book**

I was driving my husband somewhere, late (his night vision's poor), and I punched up a CD on the car player: *Ella Fitzgerald Sings the Cole Porter Song Book*. Despite my lily-white childhood, I was raised on her voice (my mother loved jazz). I'd heard the stories, apocryphal or not, of how when Lena Horne or Lady Day or Ella (all queens of my childhood) played the big hotels, they might be allowed to sleep there but after they left, their bed linens would be boiled clean, separately from those of the white guests.

So I tensed—I always do—as the lyrics to "Miss Otis Regrets" began. *Miss Otis regrets she's unable to lunch today, Madam.* Ella sings sweetly, ironically, laved by a slight willowy background of piano. Miss Otis can't *lunch* because she's being *lynch*ed, an uncivilized substitution of vowels. Ella sings on, achingly. The CD plays on. The terrible events unspool.

It's unbelievable to me, but my husband chuckles. He chuckles again.

I am incredulous. *Do you* know *this song?* I ask. I want to give him the benefit of the doubt. He didn't grow up with this music. He was a Sephardic Jewish boy (born in Cairo, Egypt, where his Italian family had lived for generations) raised up in Cairo's British schools on British social niceties during World War II, while Rommel advanced on the city, striking terror in the hearts of its Jews. But my husband didn't pay much attention to this terror advancing. He was just a tiny boy listening to opera, where the libretto is just a wash beneath the wall of music. Even now, he doesn't always attend closely to lyrics.

Sure, I know it, he says now of "Miss Otis Regrets." He is fiddling with the temperature control on the dash. *It's sarcastic, isn't it? About how everything can go wrong but this rich woman's only sorry she won't get her lunch?* Like the folk songs in England, he explains, where the marquessa worries her stupid head about some stupid thing while her children are stolen and her manor house burns down.

How in the world, I marvel, has he managed to pluck Brit satire from what has always been to me American black pathos?

It turns out all he is hearing of Ella's plaintive paean are the absurd "luncheon regrets" lines. So, huffily, I explicate for him the layers of tragic irony: a black woman lynched for killing her white lover—a woman whose defiant RSVP of regret on her death-tree (*the old willow 'cross the way* from the jail) is that she can't attend Madam's luncheon—one she'd never be invited to in any case, except as the black "girl" to serve the ladyfingers.

I am so sure that "Miss Otis Regrets" is an indictment only slightly less gut-wrenching than Billie Holiday's "Strange Fruit" that I finish our errands quickly and race us right home to prove it. I plunge straight into research. No way can "Miss Otis" be just Cole Porter's sardonic riff on some ancient political ditty disguised as nursery rhyme where Milady flits around in her frippery while the monarchy is overturned and her children are dragged away to the Tower (e.g., "Ladybug, Ladybug, fly away home; your house is on fire, your children are gone"). I am a putative white liberal confused about race relations. I lack simple instinct for what to do. It feels too slow, after centuries of neglect, to just let race relations pan out as they will; but it feels like artifice to try to *work at* them, like a fevered sifting to get to gold.

I play no part in race reparations. By "reparation" I don't mean cash payouts or dedicated real estate—the equivalent, at last, of the carpetbaggers' promise of 40 acres and a mule; I mean finally treating people *naturally*, without considering their race. In my own lily-white childhood up North, I knew no black people. Now, in North Carolina, I still don't. Two of the black families in our neighborhood have planted For Sale signs in their yards, and I feel bad. I'll never know if they're leaving because they felt unwelcome or simply because, like everybody else who moves from here, their careers require them to go. But if they did feel estranged, I did nothing to make them feel at home. Maybe if I'd talked to them?

Though I can't make small talk to save my life and so rarely say a word to any neighbor, white or black, my silence toward my black neighbors looms worse in my mind. If I do say some-thing to a black neighbor in passing, it sounds painful, studied (because it is). I wish for the day to come when a person's race won't register so sharply with me. But I'm not there yet. Often, if I try a friendly nod at a black person out in the world, I read in his or her face hauteur, disdain, anger, disgust, *Keep Off!* But that may be only my own expression mirrored at me: My friends and family claim that *I* always look angry, judgmental, or supercilious.

My very nature is odd: I peer in fascination at anyone not like me (I mean this in a good way because I'm truly interested, in my too self-conscious, diffident way—but my friendly interest comes off wrong). So I have to monitor myself and not stare when I see black couples out taking the air in our neigh-borhood. Interracial couples (three live here) are even more enthralling to me—I admire their bravery as they bridge two worlds, enviably blending (as I see it) Edenic innocence and chutzpah. But maybe I'm projecting all this, out of my knee-jerk tendency to simply invent lives not like mine. Maybe they're just two people in love out walking, simple as that, and the constant bridging-and-balancing act between their two races is all in my head.

My uneasiness with race causes me great spinal rectitude. I'm stiff. I fear the least pea of racial humor. At age eighteen, in my university library up North, I found by accident my first small volume of Alice Walker's poems. Her line noting a man's "feet of clay" stuck in my head like an icon—a vision of feet literally sucked down into Southern clay. I considered her a serious woman. Over the years, I read more of her work, but missed out on her novel *The Color Purple*. I was stunned when, in 1985 (I lived in North Carolina by then), my date and I sat in a theater and the black audience watching the film version around us roared with laughter throughout. *Co-opted and twisted*, that's what they are, I thought grimly. Co-opted and twisted by centuries of oppression. I saw the film on television later (by then I'd also read the book) and could concede there was a *little* bit of healthy wit and slapstick amid the abuse.

I am pleased to report (smugly) to my husband that in all my research I can't find a thing about English ballads as source: "Miss Otis Regrets" is not about a marquessa. I find instead that, possibly, the lyrics were penned by Cole Porter (in 1934) for his friend Ada "Bricktop" Smith—a black woman from West Virginia with brick-red hair renowned throughout Paris for her flamboyance as the owner of the cabaret Chez Bricktop. This proves to me that Porter, writing lyrics for a black woman from the American South, intended "Miss Otis Regrets" as an indictment of black lynchings.

But then I find that Porter never said he wrote the song for Ada Smith (*she* said it) and its first recorded performance was on the London stage, sung by a white man, Harold Byng, or Bing (no relation to Bing Crosby), in a drawing-room farce called *Hi Diddle Diddle*. Like its silly name, the play poked fun at white high society—no race element extant. The high-society satire (with an anti-Wagnerian, anti-war overlay) was reprised in 1943, starring Pola Negri (Polish and white, despite her vaguely race-evocative last name). So, no race element there, either. And William McBrien's biography of Cole Porter never mentions race as an issue. According to McBrien, Cole Porter claimed that "Miss Otis" was born when he was perusing the social register one day, saw the name Otis and decided to have some fun. Presumably at the expense of white ladies on the register. Porter furthermore added something to the effect: *You've never heard it sung until you hear Monty Woolley sing it.* Woolley, of course, was Porter's good friend, a haughty comic actor who gave everything his (Woolley's) signature snobbish, arrogant twist. But again, no race element there.

Besides Ella's famous version, the song has been recorded by dozens of people, many of them black but certainly not all, including Nat King Cole, Cab Calloway, the Mills Brothers, Fred Astaire, Rosemary Clooney, José Feliciano, Bette Midler, Linda Ronstadt, Bryan Ferry, and Kirsty MacColl/The Pogues. That last collaboration melds "Miss Otis Regrets/Just One of Those Things," so it may in fact be a light version (though MacColl's reputation is for sad songs).

I haven't heard these other renditions so I can't attest as to whether they're up-tempo or as achingly plaintive as Ella's. But I'm sure that she, for one, could not possibly have been just goofing when she sang it, her voice brimming with heartbreak. I couldn't respect any treatment that wasn't tragic.

Maybe my dead-serious sense of it *does* rise from my own white liberal guilt at race relations in this country. Maybe if I would just lighten up I could get the joke, too. But, despite Cole Porter's disclaimers, despite his seeming to toss up lynching as a joke, the lyrics beg for, they insist upon, more than a chuckle. Maybe his serious shadow side wrote the lyrics without him, as it were? Whatever he intended, in my mind, "Miss Otis Regrets" is a dirge and an indictment.

I'm not the only one for whom the song is a conundrum: *If it's just a silly satire, why does it feel, instinctively, like so much more?*

One aficionado (unidentified, posting on an Internet site devoted to the song) says:

> *The series of events in the lyric is, to a modern eye at least, ludicrous.* [I assume the writer means that lynching is now to be laughed at as absurd because it doesn't happen anymore, rather than that lynching is a giggle.] *It was probably ludicrous at the time when Porter wrote the song* [actually there were 24 recorded lynchings of blacks in 1933 (see Zangrando), the year before Porter wrote his lyrics], *although of course it is not unknown for social inferiors (blacks or women) to be dealt much harsher punishments for harming their so-called betters than it would be the other way around. . . . These are political issues, feminist issues almost— an unexpected depth in a shallow little musical number which I suspect has rather contributed to its enduring popularity.*

Although a promised Broadway show has, of this writing, failed to materialize, industry buzz a few years back said that Fantasia Barrino, the 2004 *American Idol* winner (a savvy and talented young black woman from High Point, North Carolina, just down the highway from me) who advanced to Broadway as Celie in *The Color Purple*, might be tagged to play Ada Smith in a Broadway production called *Bricktop*. Wouldn't she have to sing "Miss Otis Regrets" if Ada Smith claimed it was written for her? Wouldn't the race element *have* to figure?

So while some say the message of "Miss Otis Regrets" is meant to be sung by the white servant of a high-society white woman, I will never believe Miss Otis was meant to be merely a silly white woman for whom getting herself hanged is a faux pas, simply *inconveniencing, darling,* another woman who now will lack a fourth for bridge. Though mourning a black woman's lynching may be a wrong-headed interpretation, it's the one that has given the song its resonance for seventy-five years, and it's the interpretation I'll stick with.

Still, my lugubrious mourning in the abstract for the fictional Miss Otis, the black lynching victim, does not help me say hello to my black neighbors. In my failure to be anything but a drama queen about race, wrapped up inside my overblown concerns and complete discombobulation in the face of real people, I might as well be Miss Otis myself—the ignorant, emotionally clueless, society white woman Miss Otis.

SOURCES

William McBrien, *Cole Porter: A Biography*. Knopf: New York, 1998. Print.

Robert L. Zangrando, "Lynching." *The Reader's Companion to American History*. Ed. Eric Foner and John A. Garraty. Boston: Houghton, 1991. Print. Statistic taken from the following excerpt on p. 685: "Between 1882 (when reliable statistics were first collected) and 1968 (when the classic forms of lynching had disappeared), 4,743 persons died of lynching, 3,446 of them black men and women. Mississippi (539 black victims, 42 white) led this grim parade of death, followed by Georgia (492, 39), Texas (352, 141), Louisiana (335, 56), and Alabama (299, 48). From 1882 to 1901, the annual number nationally usually exceeded 100; 1892 had a record 230 deaths (161 black, 69 white). Although lynchings declined somewhat in the twentieth century, there were still 97 in 1908 (89 black, 8 white), 83 in the racially troubled postwar year of 1919 (76, 7, plus some 25 race riots), 30 in 1926 (23, 7), and 28 in 1933 (24, 4)."

Lyzette Wanzer, a native New Yorker, currently resides in San Francisco. Her stories have appeared in such journals as *Callaloo, Tampa Review, Potomac Review, Pleiades,* the *Journal of Experimental Fiction, Iris, Apalachee Review,* and *Bryant Literary Review.* Her current work is autobiographically based, with a focus on composite and sudden fiction forms. Of prime importance to her is work that discomfits, contemplates, provokes, balances scene and summary, and delivers the unexpected in the process; the ultimate goal in her own work is to hobble the stereotypes and stagger the expectations that many have of her, as an African American woman writer. "Signatures" fits into this category. Wanzer holds an MFA in fiction writing from Mills College.

Signatures

Lyzette Wanzer

Michel Foucault must have been rolling in his grave. That, or he was winking. The order of things? A dark-skinned black bartender, old enough to be my grandfather, glasses, mustache, stately carriage, appeared in the parlor and inquired about our drink selections. Camille ordered a cabernet; I declined. Puzzled, she asked, "Isn't zinfandel your favorite?" and ordered a glass for me. I wouldn't make eye contact with the bartender. What must he think? What must he have endured over the decades, suffered, borne, to have matters come to this, to *this,* serving a black woman less than half his age in a tony parlor? This was, decidedly, a patent *dis*order of things. Helter-skelter, topsy-turvy, downside up.

———————

One cab, one zin. Clear view of the curving staircase with gleaming banister. The sofas, plush as mittens. Queen Anne graced everything else. A neat array of hors d'oeuvres on a three-tiered carousel. Camille helped herself to a small saucer of cucumber-and-cream-cheese squares—whole wheat.

———————

Beyond the introductory remarks on the landing page, the club's website had been inaccessible. All of the whitebready cargo tucked away behind a Members Only log-on screen. The intro said the club had been founded a century ago, and had a true country counterpart in the North Georgia mountains. Robert T. Jones, Jr., golf course; stables, tennis, six-lane pool. The deep end, fifteen feet.

———·———

Drinks only, Camille insisted, just try it for drinks. We don't have to eat there. They don't do cash or plastic; we'll charge my husband's account. It'll be good literary fodder, don't you think? You might use it in a story sometime. Just want you to experience it. This was Atlanta, chocolate city extraordinaire, and she was still color blind. Now, some would call that sort of vitiated vision progress, but not I. My preference? That folks see the import, see the impact, the implication of the questions they ask, the overtures they make.

———·———

She toured me around the club's five floors, wine glasses in our hands. I was most struck by the chess and billiard rooms, framed photos against dark-paneled walls showing row upon row of sartorial white males, rolls of prior chess teams in tight script, wizened parchment under glass. Camille pointed out some names with whom or from whom her husband's family were connected, descended. On the top floor, the predominately Vietnamese American staff prepared a lavish ballroom for a wedding reception. Every staff member we encountered throughout greeted Camille by name.

———·———

Still, privilege implies, often confers, a genuine inability to step inside another's skin, to borrow perspectives. We had dinner reservations at the home-cooking restaurant, west end of town. I'd chosen it because I loved fried catfish. Camille liked it, too, but called midweek to say that, when we met on Friday, she'd like us to start off at her club. She kept meaning to ask me, but it always slipped her mind, etc. Located near the downtown hub, I'd passed by or under it numerous times, an austere brick edifice, white columns flanking the double-door entrance, large balcony set with round, linen-covered tables, chairs, sometimes a polished piano, Rach concerto. I met her on the club's corner in cream chenille, *en garde*, rinsed in dread.

———•———

We returned our wine glasses to the bar. This time, I endeavored to make eye contact with the bartender, but he would not look at either of us. He took our glasses, one in each hand, an ounce of dignity for every heartbeat. My own beating so hard I could feel pressure behind my eyes, but he would not look, would not look. I was only a *guest* here; I didn't want to *be* here, I was *invited*. Coerced, almost. I am here under duress. I am ordinary, common, simple. Stop chastening me.

———•———

"Ready to leave?" she asked. I was, and proceeded from the parlor through the entry at a smart pace, several steps ahead of her. On the sidewalk, while headed to her car, we stopped when we heard music wafting from the patio. Now on the far side of 6:00 p.m., the tables filled with accoutered diners, a pianist and singer at the far end, ready to begin their set. A waiter in a white jacket saw us, on the lower walkway, gestured behind him, both arms toward the tables, the question clear on his face. So appealing and earnest, we both laughed. Camille turned to me—"You're sure you won't try dining here? With the live jazz?"—and I relented. We retraced our steps back through the parlor. The Vietnamese maitre d' met us at the patio door, seated us, handed me the single-panel menu.

———•———

The white female singer, mid-thirties, close-cropped coif, black spaghetti-strap dress, perched on the balustrade, and the pianist, a seventy-five-year-old portly Italian native. Ought to be interesting, I thought, and it turned out to be exactly that. A gentleman in crisp, unrelieved white, bow tie to shoes, moved from table to table, clipboard in hand, taking song requests. Camille requested Anita O'Day. I asked for "Love Me or Leave Me" and Billie Holiday's rendition of "All of Me." The singer didn't know either. What sort of jazz performer was she? I had no problem requesting these pieces at any number of jazz clubs in the city. Topsy-turvy, downside up, downside up.

I've become a good reader, know how to interpret body language, gestures, signals, looks, when the mouth says one thing and the body betrays the lie. I met the eyes of diners at neighboring tables, seeking hostility, dismay, suspicion. One woman grinned at me, supremely unexpected. A man did too, but his smile, only half of him in it. Ginger-seared sole was exquisite, spiced with melt-in-the mouth, nuanced undertones. The wait staff was über-attentive. The chef herself came out, long hair wrapped under a white net, addressed Camille as Mrs. Hartwick, asked how the dishes were, and what did we think of the wine pairings? She smelled of onions, peppercorn, curry.

After their first set, the duo took a break. The singer headed inside; the venerable pianist, in full-bore tux, headed to our table and, in fact, directly toward me. Inclined his head. "I know 'All of Me' and can play it, but Lana did not have the lyrics memorized and so could not sing it." Quite insistent that he was conversant with the song, with Lady Day, with Lena Horne. Sicilian residue coated his syllables. His grave sincerity made me pat his hand. We smiled at each other. He closed his eyes and nodded. The same bartender entered, presented a bottle of Pinot Blanc to the table beside ours, folded towel cradling the frosted glass. The guests leaned, as though they were on a sloping deck, to scrutinize the label. He turned to look at me. Over the pianist's back, our gazes held.

Something is awry, sir, given the humiliations, deprivations, constraints you've suffered, something is awry, so that I might even be able to enter this club; something is awry, off-kilter, about there being only we two here, in Atlanta, just us two, in a city *like* Atlanta, only we two here, just us two, and you serving me. Sir, I wanted you to know how that grabs me, that I've got my mind around that conundrum. Sir, I comprehend disorder. Grasp disarray. Recognize dissonance when I hear it. I don't have it twisted.

EYEWITNESS:
AS SEEN BY ANOTHER

*"This is a peculiar sensation, this double-consciousness,
this sense of always looking at one's self through the
eyes of others."*

—W. E. B. Du Bois (1868–1963), *The Souls of Black Folk*, 1903

Winter Seagull Toshi Washizu

Itam Jeff Fearnside

High Tech in Gaborone M. Garrett Bauman

Triptych: Paradise Gretchen Brown Wright

Born in Shizuoka, Japan, at the foot of Mount Fuji, **Toshi Washizu** never climbed his native country's highest peak. Instead, in his youth, he crossed the ocean to America. Reared in Japan, he was acculturated to that landscape, its unique atmosphere, customs, language, and history. Immigrating to the United States forced him to confront cultural barriers and to understand that someone must create his or her own sense of community. Washizu earned his MFA in film at San Francisco State University in 1983. He became a filmmaker and for decades produced award-winning documentary films, including *Bone, Flesh, Skin: The Making of Japanese Lacquer* (1988); *Mr. Oh: A Korean Calligrapher* (1985); and *Issei: The First Generation* (2000). For Washizu, the camera revealed a common thread connecting diverse cultures. Writing, he believes, is another way of looking at his world to make sense of it. Washizu's poems have appeared in the poetry anthologies *Sunrise from Blue Thunder*; *Family Matters*; *In Other Words*; *Poets 11*; *Noe Valley Voice*; and *The Walrus*. A resident of San Francisco for thirty-five years, he often travels between his two native and adoptive homes: Japan and America.

Winter Seagull

Toshi Washizu

I t was the beginning of summer 1995. Frigid fog had invaded San Francisco for weeks. In July, it cast such an ashen pall over the city that drivers turned on their headlights in the middle of the day.

On this Saturday afternoon, the streets in my Sunset District neighborhood were desolate, the pallid mists deadening the sound of traffic and occasional footsteps. I walked from my house on Thirty-Third Avenue toward Twin Peaks, along rows of ethnic restaurants and groceries, looking for sun. As I turned uphill on Ninth Avenue, a strangely familiar melody floated in the thick air, the melancholy tune long forgotten since my childhood.

> *Blue moon over the seashore.*
> *From the realm of waves*
> *a bird is born,*
> *adrift, wet wings burnished silver,*
> *crying for its mother.*

The plaintive Japanese soprano spilled from a small barbershop in the middle of the block. I peered into the window. A young Japanese man in a tight T-shirt stood in the

103

storefront, staring into foggy space. Only a few feet from me, he appeared miles away. I pushed the door open.

"Hi. Is that '*Hama-chidori*'?" I called out. He slowly came into focus and said, "You know that song? Are you Japanese?"

That afternoon, Ryuji gave me a haircut for the first time. I started going to his shop every few weeks for a trim. Each time, Ryuji would play his collection of cassette tapes that he had brought from Japan fifteen years before—recordings of a famed national diva, Hibari Misora, popular songs of the seventies and eighties, and old folk songs we had learned at school. For a brief moment, we were transported, by the music, to the land of our birth. My visits went on like this for nine months, until one day he vanished without a word, like the bird in the song to which we had listened.

"Don't know where he went. Maybe to New York. Maybe back to Japan," answered Susie, Ryuji's Filipino co-worker, when I asked for him at the barbershop.

One evening in late November, two years later, I received a phone call from a stranger named Vittorio. "I'm Ryuji's friend. He is very ill and needs someone who speaks Japanese. I found your name in his client list." That night I drove to Vittorio's downtown apartment on Geary Street.

Ryuji had been bedridden for months. His once-handsome, muscled body had become wasted, was marked with dark bedsores, and his sunken cheeks had aged him. His mind ravaged by dementia, he was increasingly incoherent. He traveled from place to place, and from one person to another in an instant. One moment he was in New York, the next in Japan, his mind roaming freely between the present and the past of ten years back, from yesterday to his childhood. He told me disjointed stories of various people, his peculiar speech a mixture of English and Japanese. I nodded an occasional "Yes, I see."

Ryuji had been estranged from his family for seven years. His ex-lover and caretaker, Vittorio, wanted to contact Ryuji's family before it was too late. He asked me to make a phone call to Ryuji's parents in Japan. I rang and a woman answered— Kinuko, Ryuji's older sister. I introduced myself, and told her that Ryuji would like to speak with her. Vittorio waited anxiously.

"Your sister Kinuko wants to talk with you," I said to Ryuji, sitting in a chair next to me.

"I know," he looked at me matter-of-factly and said, "They are here. My family came to see me, didn't they?"

"No. They are in Japan. You are in San Francisco. You are talking to them on the phone," I explained and handed him the phone.

"Ryu-kun? Ryu-kun? Kinuko speaking," said the voice of his sister. "This is Kinuko, do you understand?" Ryuji's body jolted. "Ryu-kun, what happened? What's wrong? Are you all right? Are you well?" Kinuko spoke rapidly.

At that moment crystal clarity had returned to him. "Sis? I'm not very well. No. Not getting any better. I have AIDS," he spoke coherently. "Yes, AIDS. No, you don't get better with this disease." Tears rolled down his cheeks and he began to wail like a child. Vittorio held Ryuji in his arms and comforted him.

The cold rain had eased to a drizzle when his two sisters arrived from Japan three days later. Vittorio led them directly to Ryuji's bed by the window of his small studio apartment. Propped up with pillows, Ryuji's emaciated body seemed to float in the bedding. The sisters rushed to him, and stood there in mute horror. He slowly opened his eyes from a drug-induced stupor, acknowledged his sisters with a faint bow, and calmly started talking as though they had never been separated. "Vittorio made sandwiches for you. Save some for Mom and Father, will you?"

"Mom wanted to come to see you so bad . . . but had to take care of Dad. He's too weak to travel . . . ," Kinuko's voice trailed off.

"They are looking forward to your coming home," said the younger sister Mie, wiping away her tears. Bathed in infinite silence, Ryuji looked his sisters straight in the face, with a serene smile.

At 6:20 the following morning, he let out one long gasp in his sleep. The next moment he was gone. "Only forty-three . . . ," Vittorio muttered.

Since then, his sisters have called me from time to time. "I want you to find a nice girl to take care of you," Kinuko would say.

"Won't you come back to Japan and visit us?" Mie asked.

Two years after Ryuji's death, their father, Shingo Miyazawa, passed away at the age of seventy-four.

Spring came late the year I visited Japan. In the icy March wind, the cherry trees were naked and gray. On the fourth anniversary of Ryuji's death, I was going to pay a long-promised visit to his grave in his hometown of Nagoya, two hundred miles south of Shimizu, my hometown. My brothers and I left home before dawn, their wives handing us packages of rice balls and bottled tea, waving goodbye.

My elder brothers, Taro and Makoto, took turns driving the van. As we drove south on the Tomei Highway, I noticed how heavy the traffic was, even as the city slept in the shadow of Kakegawa Summit. The round mountains were frosted green with tea shrubbery and citrus trees, orange fruit glowing here and there. We spoke intermittently about our family members, distant relatives, and old acquaintances.

The sky rapidly lightened with streaks of pale orange and pink gray. I sat up in my seat and saw Lake Hamana stretching out below, the watery mirror reflecting silver light. From the distant mountains a flock of winter seagulls came swooping across the lake. They sailed over the half-frozen water, rising with a slight quiver of the body, their wings catching the morning rays.

We arrived in Nagoya shortly after noon. The car turned off the highway into a residential area where rows of slate-roofed houses huddled along narrow streets. Occasionally our van veered to the edge of the road to let oncoming cars pass. We soon came to a cul-de-sac. Outside the wooden gate of the end house, I spotted buxom Kinuko smiling broadly, and next to her, a small elderly woman standing straight-backed, flanked by her daughters. "Thank you so much for coming from such a faraway place," said Mrs. Miyazawa, Ryuji's mother, bowing deeply. Kinuko and Mie hugged me, American style. My brothers greeted them and we were led into their modest home. A resplendent gilded Buddhist altar occupied one corner of their living room, the framed pictures of Ryuji and his father prominently displayed between two lit candles. We burned pungent incense and prayed.

After a sumptuous *makunouchi* lunch they had prepared, we walked to an age-old temple in their neighborhood. In front of the weathered wooden hall stood an ancient pine tree, myriad paper strips tied to its branches like white blossoms, prayers from past visitors. The wind had died down but the air remained chilly in the feeble sun. Our footsteps echoed on graveled paths as we entered the cemetery at the rear of the temple. A few steps farther brought us to a headstone engraved with the family name of Miyazawa, shaded and sheltered under a late-flowering plum, green with moss about its base. Kinuko poured spring water over the granite stone to purify the tomb, and offered yellow chrysanthemums she had brought. Mrs. Miyazawa handed each of us a few sticks of burning incense for an offering. With our eyes closed and hands clasped in prayer, we knelt before the tomb where Ryuji, his father, and their ancestors were buried.

Mrs. Miyazawa and her daughters insisted that we have tea at their house before we headed back home. Across the *tatami* floor, we sat facing the widow. As she whisked powdered green tea in burnished black cups with a bamboo brush, Kinuko and Mie brought out two photo albums of Ryuji. They reminisced about happy times: Ryuji at his birth, Ryuji at three, his high school days, the time when he left for America, his first home-coming, and a few photos from Los Angeles, San Francisco, and New York. They turned to the page with a photograph of Ryuji's sisters taken in Vittorio's kitchen; next to them, standing tall, was my young nephew Hiroshi. I suddenly remembered that he had been visiting San Francisco about the time of Ryuji's illness. I looked at my brother, Makoto, Hiroshi's father. His eyes were rimmed with red, his chest heaving.

"I remember him. That's Hiroshi-chan, isn't it?" Kinuko asked innocently. "How is he doing?"

Makoto could not keep his calm any longer. His stifled sobs burst out like a flooded stream. He struggled to hold it in. I rested my hand on his convulsing shoulder. Ryuji's mother and sisters were startled, but we all sat in silence for a long moment.

"He passed away last March," my eldest brother, Taro, spoke at last.

"Oh no," said Kinuko. "But how?"

"He took his own life."

Ryuji's mother abruptly stood up and left the room.

Mrs. Miyazawa soon returned with a *shikishi*, a formal rice-paper mat, with the calligraphy of a haiku poem. She addressed Hiroshi's father with deepest concern, "I am so sorry."

Makoto lifted his head, his tear-stained eyes gazing at her.

"My husband wrote this poem when our son Ryuji died in San Francisco," she said, handing the *shikishi* to Makoto. "I'd like you to keep it."

A winter-seagull
in a foreign land
faraway is my child.
— Shingo Miyazawa

Two weeks later I returned to another San Francisco morning, velvet mists extending to the ground. From my window the city, sky, and ocean were fused seamlessly. Like hands parting the fog, a seagull flew out of the shrouded gray atmosphere and landed on my neighbor's flat gravel roof. It rested there for a moment, iridescent in the morning light. Soon, the gull flew away into a clearing sky.

Itam

Jeff Fearnside

I met him when he came to pick me up from the Soviet-era sanatorium, a health spa where I had spent my first three days in Kazakhstan learning as quickly as possible some of the complexities of this vast country. I hadn't known a word in Russian before I arrived, and I struggled to pronounce properly my simple greeting to him and his wife Farida.

"*Zdravstvuite, menya zovut* Jeff." (Hello, my name is Jeff.)

They both smiled politely and introduced themselves, but said nothing more.

It was early June, but already hot. The ride to my new home, a village on the edge of the foothills to the snow-peaked Tian Shan (Celestial Mountains), took two hours. Along the way, Farida stopped to do some shopping. While we waited, Itam played a battered tape of ethnic Uyghur music, which I liked: the exotic melodies and driving, percussive rhythms wrapped in a contemporary pop sound.

Here, we first used the goulash of languages that would see us through the next two and a half months of my training—a mix of Russian, English, German, and gesture. Itam had studied German at university many years before, and I had taken a semester of it nearly as long ago. He had picked up some English from his two sons who were studying it, while I took Russian lessons every day.

He always spoke slowly and clearly to me in Russian, which I appreciated. But, like many people, he also had the peculiar habit of speaking extremely loudly, as if sheer volume would somehow help me understand better.

"Jeffrey, come!" he boomed at mealtimes, his light green eyes laughing. "*Kushai, kushai!*" It would become a familiar refrain—eat, eat!—along with *chai pei* (drink tea) and *chut-chut*. Literally, *chut-chut* means "a little," but in Kazakhstan there's no such thing as a little when it comes to food or drink. Though Kazakhstan is a Muslim country, much of the population drinks, perhaps a hangover from Soviet times. While Itam occasionally enjoyed vodka, he did so moderately, and he never pressured me to join him.

I called him my host father, but he was only eight years older than I, so he was really more like a protective older brother. He taught me the finer points about local customs, gently chiding me for shaking water from my hands after I washed them (Uyghurs believe this brings misfortune) and showing me how to give handshakes the Central Asian way— lightly but warmly, with free hands holding each other's forearms to show respect.

When I discovered that I had forgotten to bring a handker-chief with me, he gave me one of his. In every way, he made a special effort to include me in his life and the life of his family.

"Jeffrey!" he boomed. "You, me, go *arbeiten*." He always used the German for "to work," though I understood the Russian—*rabotat*—just as well. He was a veterinarian, and I once watched as he peered into cows' eyes, administered shots, and rubbed ointment into their sores.

On another occasion, he and Farida had me dress in my best for a Uyghur wedding.

Ethnic Uyghurs trace their roots to the primarily Muslim Xinjiang province of China and are closely related to the Turkic peoples of Central Asia. This wedding featured some folk music similar to what I had heard on my first ride with Itam. They also played Russian rock and roll and, more than once, the extended live version of the Eagles' "Hotel California."

At first, I felt shy and resisted invitations to join in the dancing. I sat on the periphery and watched, enjoying the seemingly bottomless portions of heavily mayonnaised salads and appetizers that were a full meal to me, though they were really just the warm-up to the actual meal. Eventually I was moved to join the happy throng, the men in suits, the women in glittering dresses, their arms gracefully twining and untwining above their heads. We danced all through the evening and into the next morning.

The days moved slowly that summer in my village. It wasn't exactly a place that time had passed by, but certainly only fingers of modernity had managed to slip in under the blanket of time. My family had electricity and a television, but, like most of their fellow villagers, no telephone. Water had to be carried from a well half a kilometer away; hot water was made by boiling it or, for outdoor showers, by leaving a barrel exposed to the sun all day.

The family's fortune, if counted in hard currency, was a trifle. Itam's income barely met their needs. But as with Central Asian peoples since before recorded history, their real wealth was measured in the richness of their family life and in animals—in their case, sheep.

Toward the end of my stay, they needed to sell five sheep from their flock to pay for the education of their children—sons Malik and Adik, daughter Takmina—for the coming year. I was invited along to help catch the animals. We hopped onto a small horse-drawn cart and slowly clopped up the road to the pasture where two *pastukhi*, or shepherds, were overseeing the common herd. Itam's father-in-law, who knew the exact age, sex, and condition of each of their animals by sight, chose the best from among them. Itam and his sons and I chased them down, tied them up, and placed them in the cart.

Clouds of dust rose into the sky, the sun fell toward the horizon, and the nearby mountains faded into a hazy blue and then an indistinct shadow. It was dark when we rode back down the road toward home. I felt bad for the poor sheep lying next to me, but I felt good knowing that we were taking part in a cycle of life that had been played out for centuries here—knowing that Malik and Adik would be able to continue studying English, that Takmina would gain a marketable skill in learning to cut and style hair before eventually going on to university as well.

I also sensed that Itam was proud of me for helping his family in this way. My feeling about this only increased on his forty-fifth birthday, the first and only time I ever saw him drunk.

He came in late for dinner, having been out celebrating with two friends from his university days. While Farida ladled out soup and prepared a pot of strong black tea, Itam rambled on, more emotional than usual. His family, unaccustomed to this, largely remained quiet. Finally, he put down his spoon and looked directly at me, struggling for words.

"*Moe serdtse* . . . ," he said at last, pressing his hand to his chest. When I said I didn't understand, he repeated it in English.

"My . . . my heart . . ."

I was touched. He was trying to tell me how much he would miss me. I placed my hand on his forearm and squeezed.

My training was over, and the time to leave for my assignment as a full-fledged Volunteer had arrived. All the family came to see me off, all except for Itam. He had planned his vacation for this time and was away again with his university friends.

I tried to give back Itam's handkerchief, but Farida refused, saying that I would need it. She also promised that Itam would meet me at the train station.

To my disappointment, he never showed up. But I left with hugs from the rest of the family and more memories than it seemed two and a half months could possibly provide.

After a fifteen-hour train ride, I arrived at my new home, Shymkent. Far from being the dangerous place I had been warned of ("Texas" my family called it, for they believed it was like the Wild West), I found this sprawling, low-rise city colorful and friendly. Its tree-lined streets were cool and dotted with many interesting ethnic cafés. The university where I would teach was small, but its students were enthusiastic. I looked forward to a bright two years of work.

This exciting time was darkened by some terrible news: Itam had died the day after I left. Previously unknown to everyone, he'd had a heart condition, which became lethal when combined with his recent celebrations.

I remembered him talking of his heart and was shocked to realize he had been trying to tell us of feeling pains in his chest. In hindsight, it seems we might have caught this, but at the time it was the furthest notion from our minds. He was middle-aged and seemingly in perfect health. Only days before I had wrestled sheep to the ground with him.

I learned another hard lesson in hindsight when I found that I didn't have a single photograph of Itam. I had photos of the rest of the family, my Peace Corps friends, some village children, my pupils, even a few random pastukhi. I must have assumed that Itam would always be around, that I would have plenty of chances to catch him in just the right moment.

The only tangible remembrance I had was his handkerchief.

It's funny how small, seemingly insignificant moments in our lives can take on such meaning later. If I had brought a handkerchief with me to Kazakhstan, then I would have nothing to remember Itam by.

There's nothing obviously extraordinary about it. It's just a simple piece of cloth, probably bought at the local bazaar for a few *tenge* coins. Yet when I look at it, I see pictures woven into the cotton: I see laughing light green eyes and in them the reflection of lush green foothills, snow-peaked mountains, dusty pastures, hazy steppe sunsets. And darkness. But in that darkness rings the clip-clop of horse's hooves, the trill of Uyghur wedding music, a voice booming "Jeffrey!" and I feel that at any moment I might stand up and dance.

M. Garrett Bauman recently retired from teaching English and Human Ecology at Monroe Community College in Rochester, New York, in order to write full time. His work has been published in *Sierra Magazine,* the *New York Times, Yankee, The Chronicle of Higher Education,* and has been awarded first prize in four national writing contests, the latest being the short story prize by the Great Books Foundation and the creative nonfiction prize by *New Millennium Writings.* He is the recipient of two New York Foundation for the Arts Fellowships, a Saltonstall Prize, a Leavy Award, and the author of two college textbooks. *Ideas and Details* (Wadsworth/Cengage, 2012), in its eighth edition, has been widely adopted. Because of the devastation of both past history and present events, one of his most memorable writing assignments was covering the aftermath of Hurricane Marilyn on the Caribbean Islands of St. Martin and St. Thomas in the company of two hundred World War II Holocaust survivors.

High Tech in Gaborone

M. Garrett Bauman

Technological societies are not the only ones wrestling with the dilemma of establishing boundaries between development and nature. During a recent winter cold spell, we received a fat packet of letters and photos from my wife's father, Ed, who lives in Botswana, a landlocked grassland country in southern Africa. Because there's no post office nearby, he accumulates months of material before he gets a chance to mail it out. After receiving the large packet, we curled up in our snowbound house to read about his doings on the other end of the world, where it was balmy midsummer.

Ed had enlisted in the Peace Corps at the age of 55. For as long as I've known him, he never really fit into corporate, suburbanized American culture. He liked to play blues and jazz and live from day to day. If creditors hounded him, he'd move to another city. But he was a great mechanic, and Botswana needed people to install water wells, so the Peace Corps took him. His first photographs told a fable in miniature.

Photo #1: Three Peace Corps volunteers sit on benches in the back of an open truck, smiling and optimistic as they head for their initial assignment in the bush.

Photo #2: A black cape buffalo—the size of a hippo on steroids—rumbles in a puff of its own dust beside the truck— the volunteers laughing and one man gesturing at the beast as if saying, "Niah! Niah!"

Photo #3: The three volunteers cling to the limbs of a tree six feet up. Below them, the buffalo seems to be waggling its horns in a machismo celebration. Ed eventually shot it from a neighboring tree, which he shared with the truck's drivers.

Photo #4: The truck—on its back, all four tires in the air—poses for the traditional safari kill shot.

Also in the packet are pictures of the town of Kanye where Ed lives, and of adults and children in brilliant yellow and red traditional robes and NFL T-shirts, and of gorgeous scenery of grasslands dotted with islands of trees. Because Africa still has such picturesque, wild areas, people forget it is the longest human-inhabited continent. Only now is technology and modernization rapidly transforming the land. Ed's letter tells about the new construction of a Holiday Inn in Gaborone, the capitol. Botswana, just north of South Africa, is genuinely friendly toward America and eager for contact, so they must have thought a Holiday Inn would make it easier for American business people and government representatives to stay there while they are helping to develop the country. They would not have to endure primitive hotels or village life.

In my father-in-law's village, the round houses are built of a mud-stucco substance and roofed with layered, long-stemmed grass so they resemble mushrooms. There's no electricity and few windows are paned with glass. This Texas-size country with Vermont's population has less road mileage than New York City, and Ed's typical garden pests are not rabbits but elephants and zebras. He tells us that when he shooed a baby elephant out of his garden, it trampled his fence to splinters.

His Christmas card is also enclosed. It pictures native-garbed people dancing to a huge, rocking boom box. It's summer there now, but Ed says when it gets cold, baboons enter the village for warmth and to catch and eat the cats. No one can keep cats for very long. If the baboons miss, the *mamba* (a poisonous snake) doesn't.

Ed keeps in shape by chasing ostrich. "Then, after a while, they turn around and chase me." He also throws rocks at the baboons to keep his arm in shape in case the American embassy in Gaborone ever gets up a baseball game like they did last year. He loves baseball news, but U.S. papers arrive weeks late and the Voice of America broadcasts only "hard" news.

"The interesting thing about the baboons," Ed writes, "is that one of them is starting to throw rocks back at *me*." He doesn't like it either that they peek into his doorway at night.

Ed's job is to install water wells and pumps in bush villages in the arid north. Until his crew arrived, women frequently hiked six hours a day, making two trips to distant springs for water. So when the water bubbled up for the first time, three-day feasts erupted. They drank, danced, sang, and told stories. He also said one chief offered him a daughter for the night in thanks, and, although Ed suspected she was one he was having "a hard time unloading," he didn't want to offend anyone by refusing her. Ed couldn't have designed a more perfect heaven for himself.

Ed plans to stay on in Botswana when his contract expires, for mechanics are prized as technological development continues. Most of his time is spent in outlying villages where life is easygoing. But once in a while, Ed gets a Western itch for modern conveniences, so he hikes or thumbs the 70 miles into Gaborone to stay at the Holiday Inn. It has a weekend special: 145 *pula* (50 USD) for a room, food, air-conditioning, pool, barbeque, and even golf. The only thing missing on the links is grass. Dry, 90- to 115-degree summers crisp American-type lawns.

At Gaborone's Community Centre, however, the Dutch embassy tested a new, super hybrid grass. It grew fantastically—which created a new problem. They called in Ed, who uncrated a shiny lawn mower as a crowd gathered. When the starter spluttered the mower to life, the crowd screamed and ran in all directions. The people returned gradually, fascinated by the grass shooting out the discharge chute. One man crawled beside the mower, grass spraying all over him as he stared into the magic chute. People stroked the crew-cut grass, lay in it, picked up the clippings, and threw them. Boys dared each other to touch the mower handle. Then the machine fired out a rock—striking the crawling man in the head. He rolled away screaming. Ed rushed over and was relieved the prostrate man was merely grazed.

"Why does he keep screaming?" Ed asked a woman.

"He thinks he's in heaven," she said. "In his religion there's green grass all around. He thinks he died and is in heaven." She laughed.

For many Botswanans, heaven does seem on the way—Coca-Colas, boom boxes, water from dry earth, U.S.-financed paved roads, T-shirts, a lawn mower. Outlying towns like Kanye may have solar hot water heaters and even some telephones. Ed has also built a few houses in his spare time, and he wires them for the approaching electricity. Botswana loves its technological big brother. The youngsters follow Ed's mowing trail like the munchkins in Dorothy's Oz. And if our paved roads lead to Botswana's diamond mines and if we use Gaborone's border location to keep an eye on South Africa, nobody asks us impolite questions. Botswanans are *nice* people.

Ed eventually found a local man willing to take over the "grass-eating machine." The recruit sweated as Ed explained the mower operation. He even started it. But when the self-propelled feature kicked into gear, the man fled in panic. The mower ran wild, scattering the crowd in terrified glee, roaring over a flower garden before Ed caught up. Somehow there was no safety shut-off. This scene was repeated for several weeks until the garden was decimated. Hilarious crowds gathered for each mowing to see what would happen next.

Ed finally hit on a gimmick that technological societies use. He photographed the man he trained on the lawn mower and fabricated an official-looking "Lawn Mower Driver's License." Courage bloomed. Soon, the driver became a haughty nabob who grinned regally as he mowed, pushing levers with the superior aplomb that computer snobs exhibit in this country. He'd flick out his "license" when introduced to people. Thus is forming Botswana's new class of the technological elite.

This is happening despite the fact that Botswana has been the most class-free democracy of any African country. Race relations are good, ambitions humble, people happy with their live-for-the-moment philosophy. It is Eden for Ed, who was a wandering misfit in the United States. And it is good work to bring wells to people miles from water, and it's humane to offer women dignity and freedom. The culture is being Westernized and modernized in good fellowship, not old colonial conquest. That's a measure of progress. But now that he's crowned a lord of the lawn mowers and wired houses for *American Idol* and reality television shows, Ed wonders if he's helping to ruin what he loves best about this gentle African country. Lately, at night, he hears the baboons moving outside, muttering, then a rock clunks against his house, and he wonders, if the cape buffalo and baboons had a vote in what the people are doing, how things would turn out.

Gretchen Brown Wright lives with her husband in Cedar Rapids, Iowa, for most of the year, but enjoys summers with the family at their lake cabin on Minnesota's Mesabi Iron Range. She has four adult children, two of whom joined the family through international adoption when they were infants. The weeks she spent in their countries of origin had a profound influence on her world view, and shaped her interest in crossing cultural boundaries through writing. Although she has experienced life on five continents and visits Guatemala twice annually, Wright is keenly aware that travel adventures are simply the first step toward understanding any culture. By keeping an open mind and listening to the many sides of an issue, she hopes to give balanced interpretations in the stories she shares. Her essays have appeared in *Adoptive Families*, *The Fertile Source*, and in the anthology *Dust and Fire: Writing and Art by Women* (2011). She earned her MFA in Writing at Vermont College of Fine Arts in 2009.

Triptych: Paradise

Gretchen Brown Wright

***P**art I: Guatemala/Sacatepéquez*
     When I first began flying to Guatemala City's Aurora Airport in 1991, a throng of beggars lingered just outside the front door, their coin pots rattling, their weathered brown palms turned upward, beseechingly, ready to accept spare change. The terminal itself showed signs of wear and neglect, and departing passengers risked their lives battling the chaos of traffic at the entrance. This introductory exposure to grime and disarray prepared travelers for what was to come.

The new century brought with it a complete airport renovation. As in Dallas, Paris, or Miami, passengers now exit safely through a high gloss hallway to the efficient passport control, an orderly, automated baggage claim, and past uniformed officials who nod as we drag our luggage through the receiving hall to the protected overhang beyond. Here we are greeted by family, friends, and shuttle operators bearing personalized placards.

Tonight my small group is met by a minivan driver, Francisco, who will take us up to Antigua. He clambers onto the roof while two young boys grunt and shove our suitcases up to him so he can rope them into place. We tried to pack light, but our bags are heavy nonetheless, and there are more of them than we intended. Although it is a Mercedes, the van now looks a little bit like a chicken bus, those legendary used school buses seen everywhere in Latin America, overflowing with passengers and belching oily fumes.

Francisco points out a few sights as we pass through the blur of busy Saturday night life in the city. We are glad to be heading into quieter territory.

"Why have you come to Guatemala?" he asks, tooting at a Toyota that tries to cut in front of him as we navigate the Calzada Roosevelt near the edge of town.

I tell him that my friends and I are here to explore different areas of the country, that we are going to begin in Antigua and nearby villages on the slope of the Agua Volcano.

"Ah! You must visit Santa Maria de Jesús," he says eagerly, nodding. "That's a very indigenous pueblo. They have some really interesting customs there. The culture is still very strong. The indigenous culture." He turns a bit, so he can interact more with me where I sit beside him in the front passenger seat. "If a couple up there wants to marry, the girl has to live with the man's family for a month. She has to cook with her future mother-in-law, and if that woman doesn't like the way she cooks or cleans or does anything, then"—he slaps his thigh— "back to her own family for her. Ha!" He puts both hands on the steering wheel again and continues. "But the man also has to live with his fiancée's family and work with her father. The same thing for him. If he doesn't work hard, or if they decide they don't like him, he can't marry their daughter." He laughs. "In another pueblo near here it's even harder. They have to live with the in-laws for three months!" He almost shouts this. "Imagine that!"

I translate for the others, and we all laugh, agreeing that most likely none of us would be married if we had been forced to run this gauntlet.

On Sunday morning we consider attending church at Antigua's Cathedral of San José, which occupies the entire east side of the central plaza; as we wait quietly for the early mass to end, we are waylaid by a very shy licensed guide who introduces himself as Edgar. He speaks halting English, and is so quiet we must crane our necks downward and strain to hear.

"Would you like a tour of this amazing building?" he asks with his head bowed, barely looking up long enough to determine if we are, in fact, interested. "It is rich with history. I show it to you now."

I remember a news article about an indigenous man who appeared in court on a minor charge to which he readily admitted, yet for which he was given the maximum penalty because he would not make eye contact with the judge. In the face of authority, the man did not recognize the difference between looking up and appearing hostile; in meting out justice, the judge could not distinguish between deference and defiance.

Edgar steps in front of us to lead the way into the sanctuary before the next mass begins. He points out the carved statues. Each has a story, though where they came from and who designed them doesn't interest me nearly as much as Edgar, who seems reverent about this crumbling structure and its sacred family of desiccated saints. There are memorials to conquistadors, bishops, and archbishops. Edgar points to each and mumbles its pedigree, the hollows of his cheeks puffing in and out as he speaks. I catch only a third of the explanation, but enjoy the moldy, limey scent of the inner rooms.

"Down these stairs is a special place. The local *campesinos* come here to pray and ask God for favors," he says with unusual vigor, pointing down a flight of worn stone steps leading to a gated black room. There are no colors here, and little sunlight, but the cause of this utter blackness has another explanation: candles. Centuries of Mayans have knelt in the cold stone of this chamber, lighting thousands of colored candles to honor saints who have morphed with their own deities. They ask for safety, health, the return of a son or daughter, success with the harvest. Small talismans lie before the black and gray statuettes and peek from niches. All surfaces in every direction are covered in layer upon layer of soot.

Outside the church itself lie the ruined foundations of adjacent religious residences that composed the original church compound, including the bathroom—once an impressive three-holed privy with running water. In the dry season, indigenous slaves were made to carry water by hand to fill cisterns on the roof so the Bishop would always have enough water to flush away his waste.

"This was considered very modern for the sixteenth century," Edgar whispers.

It was from a neighboring place of contemplation and worship here in Antigua that Sister Dianna Ortiz was kidnapped in 1989, in the midst of Guatemala's civil war. Because of her work with indigenous children in the highlands, Sister Ortiz had received letters threatening her safety, letters she tried to ignore despite their increasing malice. On the evening of her kidnapping, she had come to Antigua to pray for guidance; armed men confronted her and spirited her out of the garden to a clandestine prison in Guatemala City. For twenty-four hours she was tortured and gang raped until she was inexplicably removed from the prison by a man who spoke English with a flawless American accent. He claimed he and her captors were simply fighting Communism, and that by working with the highland Maya, she had been aiding the enemy. He advised that she forgive her kidnappers, forget what had just happened. There would certainly be unpleasant consequences if she did not.

We return to the sanctuary after the mass ends. Edgar raises an arm toward the doors.

"In the early days, long ago, the church building had nine entrances, each for a specific group of people." He indicates the main entrance with thin, gnarled fingers. "The nobles entered through the grand front doors. The middle class had a door further back." He points to a second door halfway up the side wall. "Meztizos had another entrance, and the poorest, the Indians, entered at the back." He indicates a door behind a pillar. "Now all use the same entrance, or any entrance. There is no difference now."

He looks down again, avoiding our eyes. The polish on his dusty black loafers cannot disguise their disintegrating seams or the cracked leather across his bunions. Though clean and pressed, his shirt collar is frayed and yellow, and his trouser pockets have grown shiny from hands sliding in and out repeatedly over a period of years. The tour has ended. Edgar hands each of us a signed sales brochure for a local jade factory, explaining that he receives a cut for every visitor he sends their way. When we ask what we owe him for the tour, he mumbles so softly into his worn collar that we must repeat the question twice before he speaks up. Even with a tip, we pay him the equivalent of just over two dollars for this hour of his time.

"So, this is the story about the chicken bus."

Francisco's eyes glint, and he leans forward to adjust himself in the driver's seat. He is driving me from Antigua to Guatemala City, where I will pick up a rental car for the remainder of my vacation. We have passed several brightly painted buses, all crowded, all leaving trails of greasy exhaust in their wakes.

"Most people say they are called that because here in this country, among the indigenous people, the custom is to bring with you a live animal when you visit someone. A rabbit, a duck, or, of course, a chicken. And since the people don't have cars of their own, they take the bus, the public transport. And they take these animals into the bus with them." He mimes holding a small package. "They take the chicken into the bus as another passenger." He laughs, cradling his imaginary gift. "The chickens are on the bus. It is a chicken bus."

He pronounces this /CHEE-ken BOOS/.

"That is one story, and it is the most common. But I prefer this one. These buses, they all come from the United States. They use them to take children to school. You know this? Yes. So we in Guatemala buy them, and they come down the highways from the United States all in a group, a group of yellow buses. Like a bunch of little chicks, all yellow!"

He slaps his thigh, laughing.

"And when they get here, we paint on them the names of the towns they will travel to. But the people here, they can't read. And so they wave to every bus that passes and ask, 'Are you going to my town?' And the driver says, 'No, this isn't going there. You have to wait for another bus.' And after a while this makes the bus drivers tired. They have to stop for all the people who wave at them because the people can't read."

We near the city at the beginning of morning rush-hour traffic. Grinding gears, rattling mufflers, and incessant honking punctuate his narrative.

"So they get the idea to paint the buses different colors. One town green and white, another blue and yellow. All different colors, and sometimes with shapes added to them, because the people can remember colors and figures even though they can't read. So now they are chicks of different colors."

We pass a bus painted red on the top and green on the bottom.

"This one looks like a rooster," I say.

"Oh, that's just a very old hen," he laughs. "See how rusty she is?"

A much larger bus in solid red groans past. I point to it.

"Ah! Here in the city, the buses are painted all red." He points out others, big buses in bright, sooty red. "The people call them tomatoes."

"Chicks and tomatoes," I say.

"Yes. The buses in Guatemala make a nice chicken salad."

Part II: Izabal

The road south from Flores, in the northern department of Petén, feels like the straightest in the world. We have just left Tikal, snaking beneath giant ceiba trees along a route dotted with cautionary signs depicting everything from snakes to jaguars to coatimundis. In contrast, this major national highway is a monotony of flat golden horizons. We pass cinderblock houses set back from the road in vast fields of scrub. Occasionally we see cattle, heat-tolerant Brahmans, their pale coats identical in hue to the skeletal trees I see every so often in the distance. The sky is wide here, enveloping the road, our car, and us as we pass just beyond the snag of endless barbed wire fencing.

I am traveling with my Guatemalan friend, Maria; we are on a personal tour with Pieter and Stephanie, friends from The Netherlands, who are visiting Guatemala for the first time. Pieter sits in the front passenger seat, his video camera committing this drive to digital memory. In the rear seat, Stephanie and I alternately study our guide books and doze. Maria taps the steering wheel to the rhythm of her favorite Cuban folk music CD. She is very energized today.

"I have the perfect place to take you next," she announces, glancing briefly at Pieter.

"Wherever you want to go." He winks in reply.

"What could be more perfect than Tikal?" asks Stephanie, leaning forward to give Maria's shoulder a gentle squeeze. We discussed this over wine the night before, and agree that the ancient Maya city of Tikal is mystical, magical—a safe tourist haven that has managed to maintain its aura of authenticity.

"You have your book, Greta? Look this up," Maria says, raising her eyebrows. She has a surprise in mind for us. "Look up Finca Paraiso, on Lake Izabal."

When we reach the town of Fronteras, we find ourselves in the midst of market day. Vendors line the narrow street, their tables filled with all variety of produce, shoes, and tall stacks of denim jeans. Children, oblivious to traffic, toss plastic balls, and filthy dogs doze just beyond the reach of passing pedestrian feet. Maria turns down the music; we are engulfed in purposeful chaos.

A tall bridge ahead spans the Río Dulce, but our car turns right before we reach it. Within minutes we are beyond the bustle of commerce, surrounded by acres of banana plantations. To my Midwestern eye, these tall plants look like palms, their rough trunks shooting skyward and crowned with leafy fronds. Below the greenery dangle the fruits themselves, though we can't see them. The long, phallic hands of bananas are hidden beneath bright blue plastic bags.

Guatemala, of course, was one of the original "banana republics." United Fruit Company (now called Chiquita) has long controlled much of the arable land here; its influence on regional politics hinges on its own bottom line interests, which seldom include such factors as worker health and safety. In order to produce the firm, yellow bananas we all love, massive amounts of herbicides must be applied to eliminate unwanted ground vegetation. Fertilizers are required because bananas have high nutrient requirements, and weathering and overuse of the earth have resulted in inadequate soil conditions. Fungicides are sprayed from above; other chemicals are applied directly to the base of trees. Many of the agricultural chemicals used in Central America until recently had been long banned from use in the United States. Plantation workers, toiling in conditions of high heat and humidity, suffer from headaches, eye inflammations, and chronic respiratory problems. They receive little training in the proper handling of dangerous compounds, and are not mandated to comply with safety regulations that are standard in developed nations.

"What's with the bags?" I ask over Pieter's shoulder. "They look like blue plastic jock straps."

"Those are to protect the bananas from bugs," says Maria. "The bags are treated with pesticides. The companies protect the bananas, but not the workers," she adds.

After a couple of wrong turns, we bounce down a rutted drive, past golden fields and thatched-roof houses, and arrive at a rambling collection of wooden beach bungalows. Maria disappears in search of a manager so we can register for the night; when she returns she has the keys for two of the cabins. Each has two double beds, a bathroom, and features a small porch with bright teal pillars and a cotton hammock. Lake Izabal is only steps away, glowing in the late afternoon sun.

"Finca Paraiso is back the way we came, just off the main road," Maria tells us. "We'll have to change into our swimming suits quickly. I think the park closes soon."

We are hot and sweaty after our long drive. With a last fond glance at the lake, its surface glistening in the late afternoon sun, we crowd into our hot car and retrace our route to the main road. A short distance away, on the opposite side, is a rough wooden building, the entrance to Finca Paraiso. We crunch to a stop in front as a young man in khaki uniform emerges. Arching his back to stretch, he reminds us that it will be dark soon, that we might want to consider returning tomorrow. Maria laughs and says that we are too old to swim for long, so he shakes his head and waves us through, indicating that we should follow the winding driveway into the forest.

A river gurgles off to our right, below the short bluff lined with mossy trees. I can hear it through the open window. In a few moments we find ourselves in a makeshift parking lot—a mud-packed clearing, where a wiry man in rubber boots uses hand motions to indicate where we should park. While Stephanie, Pieter, and I clamber out, Maria negotiates guide services with the man. He is quickly joined by another man, as well as a gaggle of children ranging in age from toddlers to preadolescents. The older youths carry baskets of sweet breads and nuts they hope to sell, while the younger ones just call out earnestly.

"My mother made this bread just this morning," says one.

"Please, buy from me!" shouts another.

"Señora! Señora! Señora!" the littlest cry, doing their best to be heard above the older, more insistent voices.

But we are not in a position to make purchases now. "I'll buy when we come back," I promise. "Later," I tell each child, supposing they are selling their wares together. Undeterred, they continue to shout for us until our guide leads us onto a path beside the river and they are left behind, out of earshot.

The air is pungent with the vegetal aromas of ferns, leaves, and mold. Our sandals slide across the slick mud, and our toes stub into tree roots and small stones erupting at random everywhere along the track. We are not watching our steps. To the right is the river, and in it we see women at work with their laundry, using boulders as washboards, rinsing their skirts and trousers and blouses with practiced swooshes in the deepest pools. Naked children giggle, splashing each other, floating belly up or face down in the stream. We pass a group of young men swimming in their underwear; they become silent when we approach, and follow us with wary dark eyes until we are out of sight.

"There it is," our guide says, pointing down a steep embankment.

With Maria in the lead, we scramble to the bottom, each of us lending a hand to the one behind us so no one falls. We have arrived in Paradise, a bend in the river that has, through the millennia, become a deep, clear pool. Thick mist hovers above the surface, swirling upward on air drafts like ancient Mayan *wayob*—soul companions—dancing to create their sacred space. The pool is spring fed by a cascade of hot water pouring down over calcified rock formations such as I have only ever seen before deep inside caves. We plunge into the pool, dunking our heads, kicking our legs, and sliding gracefully through the water like the little fish we try to avoid; they seem to enjoy our bread-white skin, and nibble even our most sensitive body parts. Laughing, we pretend to wash our hair in the heated rush of the waterfall. We demonstrate to each other our best floating skills, and all join hands to make a human chain that spans a section of the pool. For peaceful, thundering minutes we don't worry, don't think about our passports unattended on the shore, or the fact that no one but our guide knows we are here. This is our moment in Paradise. We have no doubt that we are in a sacred space.

But then we notice our guide tapping his wrist. The sun sets promptly at six o'clock in Guatemala, year round. I am often fooled because there is no obvious dusk to remind me—just light, then no light. It is time for us to get dressed and go.

As we stumble back along the trail to the car, our guide tells us that he and his friend depend on tips for their security services. This is their primary job, the main source of income for their families. Because they are essentially self-employed, there are no days off, no sick leave, no health benefits. Tourism is their primary source of income. And though he does not say so, we assume at least a few of the children waiting for us in the parking lot are his.

They swarm us as we emerge from the trees.

"Remember, you said you'd buy my bread!"

"No, no! Buy mine! You promised!"

"You said you wanted nuts! I saved them for you!"

So much shouting. It is impossible to tell whose voice is whose.

Maria pulls me aside. "We need to pay the guide, and his friend who watched the car. Do you have any cash? I have only this much." She pulls out a ten quetzal bill, which converts to just a little more than a dollar. Stephanie, Pieter, and I pool our bills and coins with Maria's to make two even amounts for the men. They accept them with firm handshakes and quick nods of the head. Then the children swarm us, five or six encircling each adult tourist, their small hands thrust upward into our faces. There is no more talk of banana bread or cashews for sale; they want the money we promised. I have only a few centavos and one U.S. dollar bill remaining in my wallet, not enough to go around. Stephanie and Pieter are low on cash, too. We begin doling out our small change. I choose to give mine to the quietest children. One boy appears to be mute. He grunts energetically, pecking the palm of one hand with the index finger of the other. A larger girl pulls him back, away from me, and motions vehemently to him with a type of sign language as she takes his place in the front line. He scowls at her, then crouches down and pops up again in front of her. I hand him my last cash—the one dollar bill.

"You promised me!" the girl screams.

"You promised you would buy from us!" A chorus begins, all the children grabbing and scratching and pleading. "You lied! You are bad! You promised!"

The four of us glance about wildly. We make a dash for the car and squeeze through the front and back doors, opening them just wide enough to gain entrance. The two adult men are nowhere to be seen; the children swarm the car, pounding on the windows, not backing away as we put the car into reverse and carefully inch our way out of the parking area. We can hear them shouting long after we return to the open.

At dinner, we swat no-see-ums while drinking cold beer and eating local shrimp. The restaurant is quiet tonight, so the staff has time to relax. Maria chats with them as they wipe down the neighboring tables. Most of them come from communities quite far from Finca El Paraiso, places where there is no work for them. They feel lucky to have jobs, lucky to be allowed one day off a month—sometimes—when the hotel isn't busy.

Part III: Sololá

"For once the government got it right."

Maria, Stephanie, Pieter, and I have discovered a small hotel on the shore of Lake Atitlán. The proprietor, a petite blond woman of indeterminate age, is from Austria. While serving us the third course of a delicious five-course meal, she overhears a comment made by one of our fellow diners—that the Guatemalan government had made another ridiculous decision by implementing a program promoting the use of propane in the villages lining the shores of Lake Atitlán, in the Central Highlands.

"When we first came here twenty-two years ago, the area behind us was all forested. The adjacent slopes were all forested, and Dutch tourists came to walk along the orchid trail. That's what we called it, the orchid trail. It was so beautiful." She adjusts the candle in the center of the dining table that all the hotel guests share.

"But little by little the trees were chopped down for firewood. The villagers all cook with wood, of course, and everyone has a sauna—a bath hut for washing—and they use quite a lot of wood. Deforestation of these mountains is a big problem."

The idea to promote the use of propane is sound in theory. Kitchen stoves and bath huts require great quantities of wood.

Where once villagers might have made do collecting fallen branches and other dead combustibles, the population has grown and the needs for firewood have increased. Keeping the home fires burning has necessitated the destruction of living trees and risks altering the ecology of this pristine region. Propane cook stoves have the potential to minimize deforestation.

They come at a price, however. Wood is obtainable for free and is, for the time being, at least, relatively easy to find. Bottled gas must be purchased regularly, brought by boat to the villages from Panajachel, which connects by road to the rest of Guatemala. In a part of the world where a majority of the local inhabitants live far below the poverty line, such fuel can only be seen as an unnecessary expense. One more commodity the average campesino is unable to afford. Another attempt by the privileged to improve the impoverished *indigenas* through cultural change.

"My husband and I bought thousands of small trees one year and planted them on the slope behind our hotel," our hostess continues. "We planted more where the orchid trail had been, and we gave small bottle gas stoves to all of our employees to discourage them from cutting down the trees. We told them that if they didn't like the stoves we would buy them back." She frowned. "Within a month we had bought back all of those stoves. The ladies said they were only good for cooking coffee or warming things up—they didn't make good tortillas. Tortillas need the aroma of wood smoke to taste good."

The Maya named this lake *Atitlán*, the place where the rainbow gets its colors. The local *huipiles*—women's blouses—are woven in shades of teal, blended with white and royal blue, on a black background. The line of color woven into the *corte*—just below the hip of these traditional skirts—is teal, too. The patterns are rectangular—layer upon layer of interconnected parallelograms. Some use zigzags running vertically, the points facing to the sides, like waves. I would have thought triangles, to represent the three volcanoes dominating the skyline: Toliman, across from us at this hotel; San Pedro; and Atitlán, both further down the lake. But the plane of the lake seems to be the focus here, its broad flatness overpowers the steep mountains that surround it, enclose it, defy the cone it once was in an age so long ago that only the rocks remember.

The *xocomil* arrives with the sunset. *Xocomil*—the K'akchiquel word for the wind that flows over the water and takes away the sins of the day. The hostel dining room overlooks the lake, yet we cannot see the far shore. When the *xocomil* blows in, it brings with it a heavy mist that obscures even the mountains. Perhaps sin is not really washed away at all, but only hidden in these clouds.

"The door to your bungalow is wide open," our hostess informs me. "My husband just came to tell me. I only hope all your things are safe." The tranquility here has lulled me into thinking this might be Paradise. But we are humans, incapable of living in Paradise. I hurry to check, and although nothing is missing, doubt lingers.

Over dessert, one of the hotel guests tells about her freshly broken arm, its temporary cast still chalky and around her swollen fingers.

"I don't have this because I like to break my arm," she says in accented English. "It is not a pretty story."

Her name is Carmen. Another Austrian native, she has lived in Mexico for fifteen years. Tall, sun-worn and hardy, she is used to living without the comforts enjoyed by those of us who live in what we like to think of as the developed world.

"I wanted to see smaller villages," she continues. "I was told to travel by boat three or four villages down, to where it was safe, but I got off at the second village and climbed up the hill there to see the view of the lake. It was breathtaking, and I was glad I did it. But on my way down a young man suddenly appeared in front of me, and he had a knife." She holds an imaginary blade in her good hand. "Another young man came out of the brush behind me. I was so scared! I could only think to run, to run down that hill and scream as loud as I could. They followed for a bit, but I ran very fast, and they disappeared." She rubs the rough plaster and gauze of her cast. "But I fell down and rolled over a few times. I was never so scared. Many people came out of their houses then, because I had made so much noise."

The *xocomil* blows throughout the night, sending leaves

scampering across our tin-roofed bungalow like a family of squirrels. One loud bump wakens me from a dream of capsizing boats and drowning in brilliant, teal-tinted water.

Guatemala's beauty borders on hyperbole. But I cannot deny the history I know to be true. This country has one of the highest violent crime rates in Latin America. For thirty years the country endured a civil war that bred military intimidation and political repression, and ultimately spawned a sense of mistrust still palpable more than a decade after the 1996 Peace Accord. Even now, exploited *campesinos* and *indigenas* participate in acts of civil disobedience to make themselves heard; the police and military resort to violence as a means of silencing opposition. Security forces are overworked, underpaid, and inexperienced. Travelers on rural roads regularly risk being attacked by armed bandits at makeshift road blocks. Kidnappings, political retaliation, and theft are so rampant that well-armed and well-organized perpetrators have little fear of ever being caught.

Our group eats breakfast beneath the trees above Lake Atitlán. Strong black coffee, home-baked bread with three varieties of local jam stewed from fruits plucked fresh. A halo of puffy clouds encircles the peak of Toliman; small flat-bottomed boats bob on the water, the boatmen casting nets, rowing, and pulling the nets in again. Several years ago the government decided to stock the lake with black bass to promote sport fishing for tourists, but the black bass soon dominated all other species until they were the only fish remaining.

"Pana!" shout men from *lanchas* motoring past along the shoreline. These covered *collectivos*—commuter boats—adhere to a vague schedule, but don't usually depart until enough passengers board to make the trip profitable. *Lanchas* connect the small lakeside communities to Panajachel and to the paved roads that link Lake Atitlán to the rest of Guatemala. By day, scores of tourists from all over the world come to visit these picturesque villages, dine al fresco in small garden restaurants, and, of course, to shop for textiles and beadwork sold from shops, fences, and small kiosks everywhere. Smiling children hawk fruits and homemade breads for pocket change. Young men offer their services as temporary guides. They will show you the village and help you bargain for souvenirs; they will direct you to the cleanest toilets and the nicest places to eat. The sun is bright, the air is fragrant with flowers, and the melodies of a hundred overlapping conversations prove that Spanish is, indeed, the loving tongue.

"Were you frightened last night?" I ask Maria.

She looks up, surprised. "That wind," she says. "I locked the door from the inside just to be sure. Can you imagine? We live like this always here in Guatemala. We never relax. We are always a little bit afraid."

THE OTHER

> *"And I say that Your Highness ought not to consent
> that any foreigner does business or sets foot here . . .
> nor should anyone who is not a good Christian
> come to these parts."*

— Christopher Columbus (1451–1506), after arriving in San
Salvador, in *Journal of the First Voyage*, November 27, 1492

Assailing Otherness Katrina Grigg-Saito

Fried Locusts Kamela Jordan

Israel: Devour the Darling Plagues Bonnie J. Morris

As a descendant of a Japanese samurai and a Southern Baptist Civil Rights preacher, **Katrina Grigg-Saito** writes about her multiracial background. She wants to take stories that seem "foreign" and mark the places where we all overlap. She is interested in otherness, in dissecting the intercultural exchanges that happen both at home and when she travels, and documents her world experiences in her online project *Being in Love There*. She has been to such countries as Laos, Singapore, Bali, and Iceland, and has lived in Tokyo, London, and Nicaragua. Grigg-Saito's essays have appeared in two *National Geographic* anthologies, and in the *Christian Science Monitor*, *Drum Literary Magazine*, *Metropolis Magazine*, the *Japan Times*, and CNN-Go. She worked as an on-camera TV journalist for NHK in Tokyo, and her work on multiracial identity has been broadcast on NPR and in an art-interview project, *Fishbird*, sponsored by the Brooklyn Arts Council. She received her MA in Journalism and Sociology as an Earhart Fellow at Boston University. Her thesis work, *Hybrid Identities*, examined the nuances of multiracial identification, and her first children's book is forthcoming from Little, Brown & Co.

Assailing Otherness

Katrina Grigg-Saito

I squeeze my thighs tight against the motorcycle seat and lean back into the wind, my braids shooting out behind me against sunset on the Mekong River. The sun is deepening to the orange of the monk robes of Luang Prabang. Here, all Laotian boys spend at least a year as a monk, shaving their heads and filing through the streets, swinging their little metal urns over their shoulders like messenger bags to beg for food. The drive continues into twilight. I grip onto the metal loops on the back of the motorcycle and find that my hands are soot-covered when we arrive.

We are searching for a cooking class, when my partner, Jonah, and I ask a small smiling man with the lithe body of a teenager where we should go. I tell him that we'll probably just stop by a local restaurant that offers classes to tourists, and he says, "No, no. That not real Laos cooking." He pauses, and breaks into a smile. "I am a very good cook, the best. You come to my house and I'll teach you cook."

Jackpot, I think, when he extends this invitation. Places are best soaked in through the tongue, sent stomach-ward, digested and incorporated into the body. To know a place is to visit local markets, order things with unpronounceable names, and eat street food no matter the time of day. At the top of the list is the communion of cooking and sharing food at someone's home. *Jackpot*. Jonah and I look at each other and grin. "OK!" He asks us in Laos what food we like best. "All of it!" we yell, running our minds over the congealed blood noodle soups, the spicy papaya salads, and the fried seaweed with sesame seeds, before whittling it down to the national dish, *laap*, "Yes! *Laap!* I want to cook *laap!*" My father, a cook, taught me to deconstruct recipes through taste and I want to know the secret to this dish. I can discern a cold minced meat, chili peppers, cilantro, and something bitter and foreign that my taste buds cannot name.

We crowd into his kitchen, which is open to the air so the smoke from the traditional coals can escape. Our host, sweet, smiling and eager, checks the ingredients, and I squat comfortably with him on the floor ready to write, as Jonah sinks and rises when his knees start to hurt.

He says we will make our favorite *laap*, and we begin.

He unwraps the meat: gamey chunks of red buffalo, and the tripe that looks like coral, white and sweatery. He hacks into it with a scratched cleaver, shredding the intestines into slices, as the knife rat-a-tat-tats off the wooden three-legged cutting board that rat-a-tat-tats on the uneven floor. There is a slight breeze through the chicken wire of his kitchen shack, and he gestures excitedly as I take notes. I start to realize I will never find these ingredients outside of Laos. And then he pulls out a clear plastic Baggie and holds it up to us, grasping for the words to explain the mysterious contents: a gray viscous fluid, with small solid pieces floating in it. It's in the kind of bag you carry home goldfish in, thin and knotted at the top. It swims through my head that this could be a Laotian goldfish gone horribly wrong, and I get up close to investigate. He says a series of words that seem to lick around a central point, that this might be the intestinal water of a water buffalo. When he finally unties the bag, the smell is enough to confirm his broken English. "Oh my god, I think it's shit," I whisper to Jonah, smile painted on.

This is not the story of the most delicious meal I've eaten.

When I comprehend that he is holding up a bag of shit, meant for eating, my body yanks back as if nearness would bring contamination. It is the muscular choreography of the "raising of the upper lip, wrinkling of the nose, and often a gaping that involves a drop of the lower jaw and tongue extension" (Rozin 398). Paul Rozin explains the gesture as a way of expelling the offending item out of the mouth and shutting down the nasal passages. I know the sensation from maggots, from the sound of vomit, from jerking away when the man on the subway is picking his nose and eating it. I know it from my run-in with the spiky and very smelly durian fruit, illegal on buses in Southeast Asia because its fragrance causes those not eating it to vomit. I am a brave and flexible eater, and was sure I'd love durian as much as my Malaysian friends. I popped a bite into my mouth. The reaction started before it hit my tongue—it felt like the fruit turned to vapor and burned down my windpipe. My Malaysian friends urged me to try one more time, howling with laughter at my contortions of disgust and how close I came to vomiting. Twenty countries, and I mark it as my one failure. The one thing I cannot eat.

But in Laos, in the suspended moment that pivots around this bag of shit, I don't want to believe *you are what you eat*. I try to keep my disgust from crawling out of the Baggie toward the arm that holds it, tainting my view of this kind man who brought us to his home to teach us how to cook. I do not want it to taint my view of the smiling Laotians we've met thus far. I feel the weight of the Western taboo: you don't, don't, do not eat shit. The alarm is thunderous. As Winifried Menninghaus says, "everything seems at risk in the experience of disgust. It is a state of alarm and emergency, an acute crisis of self-preservation in the face of an unassailable otherness . . ." (1).

An unassailable otherness. Otherness can be placed on a race, on a culture, on a religion. In religions, prohibitions around food delineate "other." Hasids cannot eat from the dishes of Muslims who cannot eat the pork of the Christians who cannot share a hamburger with the Hindus. Moral disgust at what others eat may keep religion pure, but it comes at the expense of connection, of the mirth and understanding that comes from communing around a dinner table.

Disgust separates self from other.

In those twenty countries I've seen, twenty-one including my home in the United States, the feeling of otherness is the one thing I can count on. Since I'm a mix of Japanese and white with whispers of black and Cherokee, nobody ever knows where I'm from, but they know I'm not from *here*, and *here* is always where I am. But I assail the unassailable. I cozy up with otherness. My life's work has been made in this pursuit of smudging the lines drawn around "other," and so, I'm up for eating a little shit.

I'm up for eating it, because my alarm of prejudice is louder and more unbearable than my alarm of disgust.

I'm up for eating it, and I do not say this lightly, because I love these people, and disgust and love cannot occupy the same space. Scientists who study maggots find them adorable or, at least, very fascinating. I will hold my sister's hair back when she vomits. My father still lovingly makes fun of me for picking my nose and eating it when I was three, a repeated story I still blame on his tendency to exaggerate.

Cozying up with otherness is why I travel. It's what I crave. I fall in love with the oddities and customs of a place. I fall in love with the people. When we arrive in Laos, we take to shouting *"sabadi!"*—hello—to anyone we see who is smiling, which means we are *sabadi*-ing almost everyone. We say *sabadi* as we chomp on barbequed meat threaded onto circular skewers, glazed like the maroon lacquer of a Japanese *obento* box. We say *sabadi* to the women and men selling skins with long hair still attached, crabs tied together like necklaces, and rodents stretched across sticks (I look away in revulsion and then have to look back just one more time). Every day we say *sabadi* to our fruit lady, who sells us a bag of mangosteen, little purple fruit whose thick exoskeleton can be torn into and discarded, revealing five perfect sections of a white fruit similar to lychees. The taste is a perfect balance between sweet and sour, tannic and refreshing. It cannot be replicated in a New England apple or a Florida orange: It belongs to Laos.

I collect and store these moments that belong to Laos, like the event we walk into in the hour before our cooking lesson begins, after hopping off the motorcycles. We follow our host— I have now forgotten his name, but I will call him De Chay, because my Laotian friend says it means "merry," and he was indeed ten degrees merrier than the already buoyant Laotians we had met—follow him into his home, one level, cement, with cut holes for windows.

Everyone seems to be moving, and the room is full of people. Aunties in straight silk sarongs with elaborate embroidered borders chop food and uncover sticky rice, and uncles, barefoot and laughing, sit with beers as the baby gets handed around.

In the corner, a tiny wizened woman with a bright pink shirt pulls herself onto a futon on the floor. Her arms are strong and she hoists the weight of her useless legs backward like a crab, to get herself situated. She is sharp and makes everyone laugh. "She is ninety-nine today," De Chay says, "and my daughter is nine months!"

We worry suddenly that we're crashing this old woman's birthday party; so, we smile big and try to make ourselves small, folding our legs under ourselves, and politely taking in the chaos. On an intricately carved pedestal and tray, offerings are piled in the form of a bunch of mini-bananas, bags of potato chips, a basket of sticky rice, and a whole boiled chicken, head intact. A big bottle of Lao Beer juts up like a stupa, and a pile of short white strings are draped over the edge. We add a five-dollar bill and some chocolates from Tokyo. The women sit too and we seem to be waiting for someone.

That someone bursts through the door with an entrance that makes everyone laugh and cheer, the master of ceremonies, a layperson able to officiate at Laotian rituals, and the uncle of someone, or they call him Uncle.

The ceremony begins.

He places the ninety-nine-year-old woman's hands on the tray and then motions for us to scoot up close, in front of the other family members, and we too hold the edge of the silver tray. We watch as he takes one of the white strings and ties it around her wrist, repeating a rhythmic blessing. It isn't until he ties the second string that I move my eyes from the two of them and see the whole picture, the way that her daughter is lightly holding on to the edge of her shirt, and De Chay's mother-in-law holds on to *her* mother's shirt, and on and on in this physical birth line that stretches back to the woman's great-great-granddaughter, the nine-month-old daughter of our friend. The blessing seems to zing all the way down the line. From her body, blessed with long life, using the other bodies as a conduit to reach the smallest family member.

Then, Uncle turns to us and shouts "English!" sending everyone into convulsions. He turns to Jonah and ties strings around his wrist, wishing for long life for him and "healthy and wealthy." He breaks off an indiscernible chicken part and gives it to him to eat. When Uncle turns to me, I feel a little tug and see that Jonah is holding on to the edge of my T-shirt, too. He noticed. My eyes fill, I smile. Uncle gives me nearly the same blessing and a chicken claw with a wink, saying, "Best," tying strings on my wrists and shouting, "And many children as soon as!" He translates, the crowd goes wild.

One by one the family members approach us, take our hands in their hands, and tie more white strings around our wrists. We gnaw on the chicken parts and grin and gnaw some more. I do what I can with the scant meat of the chicken foot, familiar from early morning trips to Chinatown in Boston.

Everyone has eaten, and I assume De Chay has forgotten about the cooking lesson, or that, perhaps, this was it, but then he motions us into the kitchen. His wife's eyes cut at us as we slip away, and I try to ask if we should just enjoy his family. Skip the cooking. But then I see all they've bought for us, piles of plastic bags full of vegetables from the market. I pull out my notebook.

Only a few leaves of the greens that smell like a minty cilantro are worth keeping, and he throws out the rest of the bag; "No good," he says. It seems the local market bundles vegetables indiscriminately, but he is pickier than a Whole Foods stocker in his vegetable sorting. He rolls a pile of perfect green eggplants toward me, the size of marbles, and I toss them in the colander to wash. He helps me shimmy over the giant stone mortar and I grind roasted red peppers, the kind that fills my nose with spicy anticipation, just three. Ten peppers are migraine-inducing, six are for locals, and three since he's eating with us. Having tried a five-chili papaya salad, I am grateful for this small concession.

We arrive at the bag of shit that infuses *laap* with the bitter flavor I later learn is called *piah*. "It's not actually shit, you know," Toy, my mother's friend and Laotian refugee in Lowell, Massachusetts, tells me when I get back home. "It's bile. The green stuff, right?" In that suspended moment, I don't know that the demarcation between shit and bile would have given me any comfort. The use of bile is so local to Laos, that even their close Cambodian neighbors use a special epithet for Laotians that translates as cow-shit eaters. "I would feel really terrible [if someone called me that name]," Toy tells me, "but I would say something back, I would say, it's good stuff, you should try it first."

For Toy, *piah* is the taste of home. *Piah* is the taste she craves and cannot find anywhere when she arrives in the United States. In this new country, she wonders why adults drink milk, a drink she thinks of as solely for babies, and plugs her nose at the horrid smell of American cheese.

Piah is the taste that she finds by knotting the small intestine of a cow and carefully squeezing out the precious liquid. It is a cow she buys with other Laotian refugees, newly arrived. Together, they go to a farm in summer and pool their money. One cow to share. Every part is used: the skin would be dried until it was hard as a stick and used as bullion, the hooves and lower legs would be cleaned and boiled and used for pickling, and the precious bile squeezed and divided up among people hungry for familiarity. Its bitter taste shrunk the distance from Laos to Lowell, a momentary lull in the collective ache for home.

The bile goes into the hot wok, with a healthy sprinkling of a spice from an old painted tin. "Do you want to write down the name of the spice?" Jonah asks. "Oh no, that's OK," I say. "I think I know what that one is.

"Ajinomoto?" I ask De Chay, and he shouts *yes!* We are speaking the same language now. Ajinomoto is a Japanese company and the foremost producer of . . . "It's MSG," I say to Jonah, and we try to hold back our giggles. We add the chopped tripe and meat and chili peppers and greens to the wok and we're done.

We take the trays of food out to the family, whose numbers have dwindled. De Chay's wife sits on the floor, winding banana leaves into containers for offerings for the monks at dawn; his great-great-grandmother pulls herself backward with her strong arms, under the covers, oblivious to the noise and the light.

We sit together again. It's time. De Chay opens up the sticky rice. I reach and notice my wrists, covered with string blessings.

I carefully maneuver around the ants that are devouring a corner of the rice, and take two finger fulls with my right hand, sending it first into the stew we've made, the dish that will not have the *piah* taste. De Chay is watching us expectantly and we glance to the other dish, the *laap*, its tripe glistening. I know how chewy it will be because it didn't cook long enough to soften, and I know that when I taste it, I will be able to name the secret ingredient.

"I don't know if I can do it," Jonah whispers, and I say, "I think we can."

Jonah stalls, asking De Chay about the single 10-inch hair that grows out of a mole from underneath his chin, the only facial hair he has. I wince in embarrassment, but then De Chay says with incredible pride that it is a gift from his father, who received it from his father, and that he must not cut it because of that connection with his family. He adds with a laugh that his wife hates it.

And even without hearing Toy's voice—"I feel sad that they look down on my food. My mother, my grandpa, my grandma, they eat it, I still eat it"—I feel part of this lineage, blessed and tied in. Even without her voice I want to share this with De Chay, I want to taste our friend's home and family.

I look at my partner. Our hands are holding the sticky rice. We take a deep breath and dive. Into the *laap*, spicy and cool with that now-unmistakable *piah* taste. "*Saep lai lai*," we say, delicious, swallowing a gulp of Laos: its history, its poverty, its *wat* temples, its smiling monks, its shouts of *sabadi*, its ceremonies and lineage, and the contents of one water buffalo's carefully squeezed intestine.

We dive in again.

SOURCES

Winnifried Menninghaus, *Disgust: Theory and History of a Strong Sensation,* trans. Howard Eilard and Joel Golb. Albany: SUNY, 2003. Print.

Paul Rozin, "Food and Eating," in *Handbook of Cultural Psychology*, ed. Shinobu Kitayama and Dov Cohen. New York: Guilford, 2007. Print.

Kamela Jordan grew up as the daughter of American missionaries in a small hilltribe village in the mountains of northern Thailand. Living outside her country of origin and having the identity of a foreigner in her country of residence during her formative years gave Jordan the opportunity to interpret culture from the outside looking in. She has found this perspective to be a great asset in her adult life, giving her increased objectivity regarding her own patterns of thinking and understanding for those who think differently. "Fried Locusts" was a finalist in the Preservation Foundation's 2007 General Nonfiction contest and was published at *storyhouse.org.* Jordan also won first place for nonfiction in the 2008 InScribe writing contest for her essay "A Sunday School Christmas." She currently resides in Rochester, Minnesota.

Fried Locusts

Kamela Jordan

Before you can make fried locusts, you have to catch them. Kari and I used to go out after school with Dance and her sister Mouse to where the eucalyptus and teak grew in thick stands behind the classrooms. There in the shade the air vibrated with the shrill drone of locusts singing in the tree branches. All you need to catch them is a long bamboo pole, a plastic bag, and a rubber band.

Plastic bags and rubber bands lay everywhere—colored cellophane snagged on fence posts, tan squiggles camouflaged in the dust. If we couldn't find a suitable bamboo pole, sometimes we'd go down to the paddies and dig for snails, or raid the backyard for limes to peel and eat with salt. When the mangos swelled in expectation of April rains, we picked them green and sliced them paper thin, swilling them in fish sauce and palm sugar with a sprinkling of red pepper. The sweet, sour, and salty slices slid down our throats leaving a fiery trail in their wake.

On days when it was too sultry and still to work up the energy to stalk locusts, we'd sit in the creek behind the house and drag a fine net through the mud, bringing up squirming masses of tadpoles and scrambling crabs. If Mom was too hot to work on language lessons, we could persuade her to mix up a bowl of salty batter and fry the crabs in hot oil. We ate them whole, crunching the shells between our teeth.

147

Thai school didn't get out until four o'clock in the afternoon, and sometimes Dance and Mouse had to carry water after school, or help chop banana stalks for the pig feed. If it got to be too late to hunt an afternoon snack before dinner, we satisfied ourselves with making pretend food, picking the pungent weeds that grew behind the back fence and squeezing them in a bowl of water. When we set the slick, green liquid in the sun, it turned to bitter jelly.

Kari and I only went to Thai school for half days. In the morning we put on our uniforms—white shirts with round collars, pleated blue skirts, and shiny black Mary Janes—and lined up in front of the flagpole with the other kids from Elephant Field. After singing the national anthem and holding out our hands for nail inspection, we studied reading and writing, copying row after row of the curling alphabet, forty-four consonants and nearly as many vowels.

After lunch the classes weren't quite as academic. There was naptime, and then weeding the school flower gardens, and maybe a little math. So in the afternoons, Kari and I stayed home and Mom taught us in English—more reading and writing, history, math, science. It wasn't nearly as much fun being in a class of one (my sister and I, being in different grades, were in our own "classes" at home), but on the other hand, you didn't have to worry about the bamboo switch, or about being made to sing the Star Spangled Banner in front of the whole class if you were late. Plus, I could understand everything that was being said.

When I first started Thai preschool at the YWCA in Bangkok, I didn't understand a word. I ran away to Kari's classroom and hid under her desk, and one day when the teacher dragged me wailing back down the hall, I leaned over and bit her hand. After that I was allowed—or perhaps requested—to stay home for a month, and when I went back, I had learned enough Thai from the maid that I was content to stay in my own classroom.

After a year, we moved to the wilds of the northern mountains, where the Communist insurgency simmered in the hills and helicopters rattled overhead ferrying soldiers and guns to the invisible fight. When we awoke the first morning to find the entire neighborhood crowded in our yard, chattering nervously as they waited for a glimpse of the white foreigners, I was stricken to find that the dialect was so different as to be completely unintelligible.

I sulked and stormed when Dad took me down to the school to register, but when I was sent sniffling into the class-room, I discovered to my utter relief that school went on in the same Central Thai dialect that I had learned in Bangkok. After a while, the local dialect started slipping off my tongue unbidden at recess and after school. I still didn't know all the words in my reader, but I knew enough to get by, and the words I didn't know, I could learn to spell.

And learn to spell I did, for each misspelled word resulted in a stinging lick across the palms with a bamboo switch, or with a ruler if a poor speller had tossed the switch out the window while the teacher was out of the room. You were given a chance to correct your mistakes, and then if they were still misspelled, the penalty rose to two lashes for each word. The treacherous alphabet sported five letters for the *kh* sound, four for the *s*, five for the *t*, and innumerable sneaky silent letters trailing off the ends of words, so rare was the day when someone didn't go home from school lined with angry red stripes.

With a quick memory and a high motivation to avoid pain, I was rarely switched, though sometimes the teacher called me up to the front anyway, pretending to add up my errors, just for the suspense of it. All in all, half days weren't a bad trade-off.

Kari and I finished our English homework long before Thai school let out, and we read Nancy Drew books or dressed our dolls while the chorus of afternoon recitations floated to us across the creek. Multiplication tables were chanted in singsong unison, with a high-pitched counterpoint of alphabet drifting up from the younger grades. *K is for kai, O chicken, my chicken. Kh is for khai, the egg in its nest. Kh is for khuad, this bottle of mine.*

Recitations meant Dance and Mouse would be home soon. A few other kids lived along our stony lane, but we didn't often play with them. Pem was Kari and Dance's age, but she stole our plastic Fisher Price telephone and picked lice out of her hair and dropped them into ours. Sert was a couple of years older, and although he sometimes picked tart *saton* from the spreading tree in his yard and peeled them for us with a machete, he wasn't interested in playing with little kids. We regarded Sert with a sense of awe, watching enviously as he scampered up the curving trunks of palm trees and tossed coconuts down to his mother for her curry, or shinnied down into the echoing darkness of the well to retrieve her dropped dipper.

Bear from across the street was our age, but didn't care to play with girls; he preferred to go down to the school yard and kick a rattan ball over a net with the boys from the other side of the main road. We saw him only rarely when we carried our pink nets over to stalk butterflies in his mother's flower garden. We could always find butterflies there, flitting over the riot of hot-colored zinnias and gerbera daisies, scarlet pinflowers and golden buttonflowers, crimson hibiscus and pale pink nail-flowers whose translucent petals you could lick and stick on your fingernails and then pretend you were a fine city woman with places to go.

Dance and Mouse left us on our own when we hunted butterflies. You can't eat butterflies. But mostly it was the four of us, wandering through each other's front gates after four o'clock, or clambering over the bamboo fence and plunging through the sugar cane thicket to organize our hunting expeditions.

On Saturdays after our chores were done, we were allowed to ride our bikes down the long hill to the river that ran lazy and clear in the dry season and rushed by in a red-brown torrent when the monsoons fell. The sisters snickered behind their hands when we asked permission to go to the river. They did exactly as they pleased when the work was done, and if they came home late for supper, they simply ate on their own.

Down by the river, the metallic whine of the locusts filled the acacias with their raucous din on the shady banks. In the water, brilliant green algae clung to the rocks in strands as fine as cotton and streamed out in vivid swathes in the meandering current. Kari and I pulled off thick clumps of it and draped it over our heads, pretending we were mermaids with flowing green hair. Mouse and Dance laughed and told us we each looked like the demon that slips into your window in the dark of the night and strangles you with his long tongue.

Clusters of kids from the town across the river gathered on the banks to watch the white girls play in the water. "Albino buffalo," they shouted, and sang the familiar taunting song, "Foreigners have long noses, Negroes have flat noses." Not that any of them had ever seen a Negro, probably not even in pictures, but even in the most isolated valley, every child knows the song.

When we tired of being mermaids, we squeezed our algae locks into sodden balls and filled Dance's bicycle basket with them. Back at home, we would pick out the little pieces of sticks and leaves, and her mother would put the long green strands in the evening soup.

Small fish swam in the shallows of the river, too, darting flashes of silver and brown, too quick for us to catch, even with a net, but Dance always brought her fishing basket, just in case. The basket was shaped like a vase, with a narrow neck and a wide mouth. The lid was fringed with stiff strips of rattan that pointed down into the neck of the basket like a funnel. Push your catch through the funnel, and it wouldn't be able to jump back out again. A long piece of twine threaded through loops on the basket's neck, so you could tie it to a bush at the water's edge and set the basket in the shallows where the river could flow through and keep your fish alive.

We carried the basket to hunt locusts as well, using the twine to tie it around our waists. When the swarms settled thick in the trees so that the air rang with their noise, it didn't take long to fill the small basket. They were easy prey, cocky and brash with their noisy songs that led you straight to their perch. It was easy to pick one out on a branch and sneak up behind him with your open bag tied to the end of a pole with a rubber band. You snapped the pole down over the branch, the locust flew up into the bag, and then he was yours to fish out and pop into the basket, where he buzzed loudly, a prisoner of war.

We thought little of the war that went on in the hills surrounding our unimportant little valley. The constant helicopters were just another raucous creature adding their noise to the din of the locusts. "If you don't stop crying, giant monkeys will come down out of the helicopters and eat you," the babysitter told my little sister. "Wave to the helicopter," Dad told her when she ran to hide every time the clattering noise crescendoed overhead. "It's bringing cookies to the nice soldiers who have to sleep in the jungle, far away from their mommies." At night, machine guns added their rat-a-tat rhythm to the clamor of crickets and the slow croak of frogs in the paddies.

We ate the frogs, too, scooped them up with a net and popped them down into the basket, tiny things that were best fried whole with a crunchy skin of batter, like the crabs. But we didn't have to wait for Mom's help to cook the locusts, which didn't need a coating of batter. We brought the buzzing basket home and pulled them out through the funnel one at a time, snapping off their legs and wings and rinsing them in well water. In Dance and Mouse's kitchen, we knelt and blew life into the embers that smoldered in the ash pile of the charcoal stove. It only took a moment for the oil to sputter in the soot-blackened wok and another moment for the locusts to hiss and pop in the heat. We sat on the back steps and ate them in the waning afternoon heat. They tasted like popcorn, crisp and salty and greasy, and a little like earth.

A women's studies professor at George Washington University, **Bonnie J. Morris** is also the author of eight fiction and nonfiction books, including three Lambda Literary Award finalists—*Girl Reel* (Alyson, 1999), *Eden Built by Eves* (Coffee House, 2000), and *Revenge of the Women's Studies Professor* (Indiana, 2009)—and *Women's History For Beginners* (2012). "Israel" won Jane Stories Nonfiction Contest, and Morris's essay "The Writing Sensibility" appears in Diana Raab's *Writers and Their Notebooks*. Having kept a journal since age twelve—now on notebook #162—Morris regularly publishes travel narratives, food memoirs, and cultural essays. She uses eyewitness descriptions from her older journals, and draws from time spent living in the Middle East and as a faculty member of the global Semester at Sea program. Morris earned her PhD in women's history from the State University of New York at Binghamton, and as a visiting research associate at Harvard Divinity School, she taught Harvard's first graduate seminar on Hasidic women in America. Currently she serves as scholarly advisor to the National Women's History Museum being built in Washington, D.C.

Israel: Devour the Darling Plagues

Bonnie J. Morris

Delicious dark chocolate! Seder tray comes in a reusable basket—maybe like the one in which baby Moses was discovered. The kids are sure to giggle—and shiver—as they devour the darling plagues.

> — "Chocolate Seder Tray and Chocolate Plagues," *jewishsource.com*

It's come to this: *chocolate plagues.* Each year at Passover, Jews throughout the world retell the biblical account of the flight from slavery in Egypt over two nights of ritual meals; and central to this holiday is the memory of the ten plagues God visited on our enslavers. But now some inventive candymaker has cast the plagues in chocolate for dessert, turning sorrow into sweetness for the younger generation. Thus, the search for nouveau kosher Passover desserts led the macaroon-weary out of Egypt and into a gourmet Promised Land. What could be a better metaphor for the entire history of Israel?

Sorrow and sweetness, food and violent diasporic upheaval—these are entwined throughout Jewish heritage. The flight from slavery is symbolized in a flattened sheet of matzoh; and Jewish communal separation from gentile culture, sparking so many misunderstandings across time, has roots in the dietary laws. *We can't eat your food. We can't eat with you.*

Jewish holiday foods are nothing less than flavors of

survival. Love, guilt, and matrilineality are all conflated in the image of the Jewish mother eternally overfeeding, the taste of Judaism transmuted down the motherline. But modern Israel? It's not a land of milk and honey, but of angrily thrown stones; a cuisine summed up as falafel balls and oranges; a vacation-land for zealots, a geography of war.

There is no way to deny the political heartache of modern Israel, the impossibility of finding serene perfection in bullet-strewn Jerusalem; nor is Israel the feminist utopia of old kibbutzniks' dreams. But like so many Jewish kids before me, I went. As a young idealistic student, I went. I went before the *intifada,* before the expansion of illegal settlements and occu-pations, during the optimistic heyday of the Camp David accords and a shared Sinai of Bedouin, Arab, and Jew. In those *chamsin* winds of hopeful change, I studied in Israel, the year I was twenty, in 1981. And I was one of a handful of openly gay students, living with my lover in the cockroach-strewn dorms of Tel Aviv University.

For a year, I shopped and cooked and ate in Israel. And in trying to recreate that younger, different year, my mind hurts, but my mouth waters. *I broke bread with the Bedouin. I picked zucchini with soldier girls. I bought bags of kibbutz grapefruit for five cents. My grocery list said Eshel, Meetz Paz, Garinim. I sang along to the radio ad,* "Bli Meetz Paz, ani lo zaz!" —*without my grapefruit juice, I don't go anywhere!* "Zay tov—zay tov—zay OSEM!"

I sensed that Israel would be a food-oriented experience long before my plane landed at Ben-Gurion airport. En route, during that first long El Al flight, I marveled at the steady stream of foil-wrapped meals served to us, one hearty kosher snack after another; and when I finally pushed away a tray half-eaten, the woman seated behind me grabbed my shoulder, leaned over and cried out, "What's the matter with you? You're just going to leave that? Finish it! Eat it, already!"

I soon discovered that a nation forged by Jewish mothers—many of them concentration camp survivors—looked at food very differently than adult women in diet-conscious America. I never saw an ad, that year, featuring a *skinny* model; I landed in a society of big, tough, hearty-eating women, many of whom casually toted machine guns. Food was joy, a release from the tension of security and distrust. At the movies, prefeature commercial ads showed off sexy new refrigerators and freezers, tantalizing the audience like a striptease as double doors swung open to reveal not erotic flesh but shelves packed to bursting with chocolate and banana-flavored pudding. "OHHHHHHHH," Israeli audiences moaned. Dessert was fetish, the fridge a sanctuary of spiritual and orgasmic promise.

I found that the real "taste of Israel" was a cuisine made up of these locally produced refrigerated products, which were intended, in the best family-values way, to be eaten at home. A full sit-down meal was seldom eaten out. Snacking, to be sure, dominated public life: Tel Aviv's café society was all about how much coffee, cheap ice cream, and cheese *borekas* one could stuff down while debating national politics. But dinner you ate with your parents—or in the kibbutz dining hall. There was, as yet, no pretentious Top Chef restaurant cuisine. (As recently as 1998, world traveler Richard Sterling, writing in *The Fearless Diner,* classified Israel as "one of the world's culinary deserts" [94], ranked just after Chad and Arkansas.)

Hungry student eaters fell into two categories: religious and backpacker. For the ultra-Orthodox youth sent over from America to study in yeshiva dormitories, Samuel Heilman put it best:

> Not only were the dormitories and physical plant of these Israeli institutions frequently austere—often in direct contrast to the living conditions in America—but the diet was Spartan. Missing were the rich culinary choices of America, and in the early days (before the junk food wave invaded Israel, putting a pizza parlor within reach of every yeshiva and credit card), it was not unusual for students to return from Israel thinner and with the typical pallor of the yeshiva boy, another external sign of their transformation and their separation from the fleshpots of America. (117)

For the rest of us, the hordes of Americans, Australians, Canadians, Brits, Norwegians, and Danes with International Student ID cards laminated into our backpacks, less concerned with keeping kosher than with stretching our shekels to see the world, cheap eating had its challenges. For one thing, American product chauvinism was evident everywhere, most ubiquitous in the Hebrew Coca-Cola shirts dangling from old hangers in Jerusalem. There were always Sprite ads at the movies, soft drink banners flapping from cafés. To drink "local," one had to quaff Maccabee beer, Tammuz juice, or Tempo Squash.

My expectations were tutored by the two guidebooks I'd been given for the year: Arnold Sherman and Sylvia Brilliant's *Israel on $20 A Day*, and the Harvard Student Agencies' *Let's Go Europe 1982*, which had supplemental chapters on Israel, Morocco, Cyprus, and Tunisia. Both books reiterated a mantra of sticking with simple and local foods: pita, falafel, humus, tehina, olives, fruit, and Turkish coffee. *Let's Go* pointedly cautioned against *shwarma* meat from the too-often flyblown spit: "The quality of meat being what it is, Israelis rely to a large extent on dairy and vegetable products, especially salads and yogurts" (442), advice I took to heart during what became an essentially vegetarian year. But a salad, I learned, meant onion, tomato, and cucumber, never leaf lettuce. Feta cheese was not Greek, but "Bulgarian." Pointing and smiling worked very well with vendors, most of whom were genuinely friendly; later I learned how to bargain and how to drink coffee with Arab shopkeepers. I didn't think I'd go home pale and thin.

As a college student in America, I'd lived at home, enjoying my mother's cooking. Here at Tel Aviv University, I was in a dorm for the first time—and one without a meal plan; all students were obliged to cook and clean for themselves. Within minutes of unpacking my three suitcases for the year of study abroad, I was heading down to get groceries with the first real shekels in my hand, while two of my suitemates (who had grown up with servants, in Morocco) stormed out of the kitchenette demanding to know "Where is the maid?"

Near the campus in Ramat Aviv, close to the coastal highway (which hugged a minefield), our supermarket served an ever-hungry stream of overseas students and neighborhood housewives. The first week I shopped there, I learned the routine: bread and milk products were government-subsidized, and their prices rose on the same day the national Dan bus company fares went up; asking the cost of anything in the store led the harassed, steel-voiced cashier to throw back her head and wail "*Yaaaaaakoooov!*" which I eventually realized was the assistant manager's name; and buying slices of fresh or dried fish from the side counter wrung a snarled blessing, *"La bruit"* (to your health!) from the woman wielding the fishknife. Gorgeous mounds of bread, onion rolls, poppy-seed rolls, *challot* on Fridays occupied the right-hand side of the store—and many a time I bought a fresh loaf only to consume it entirely while walking home; I'd have to turn right around and go back for more. To go with the bread, Israelis bought not peanut butter but jars of chocolate or hazelnut spread. This was before most Americans had heard of Nutella, and the aisle of chocolate spread was another reminder that I wasn't in Kansas (actually, Maryland) anymore.

Then there was the back wall of dairy. Why it was so rich, delicious, and varied in a land with so few dairy pastures, I never understood. Milk itself looked thin and was sold unrefrigerated in bottles, unappetizing to a Western eye; but the range of yogurt, pudding, sour cream, cream cheese, cottage cheese, and fattening dessert products ran floor to ceiling, colorfully packaged, coyly named. The brand-name companies were Telma, Tnuva, and Eficol; the children's yogurt and pudding delicacies were *Danny, Yowgli*—and the ever-pleasurable *Milky.*

Milky, which still exists, offered a simple ratio of two-thirds dark chocolate pudding and one-third whipped cream top in a single-serving cup with a peel-off tinfoil lid. These bare facts don't do the item justice. Once you opened the container you had three equally luscious options: Eat the top third, the whipped cream, first? Or dig downward archaeologically, so that each bite was representational of both segments? Or perhaps the radical third alternative: mix and stir . . . ?

If I thought my relationship to product *Milky* was getting out of hand (one or two during the week, but I'd be sure to lay in a supply of two for the Shabbat weekend), I soon met other like-minded addicts. On a trip through the Sinai desert, as we went around the campfire circle introducing ourselves and our reasons for studying in Israel, I heard two ex-yeshiva boys say they came for God but stayed for *Milky.* Then, in 2003, I found this excerpt in a short story by Ruth Abusch-Magder:

> Yogurt, for example, had loomed large in my child-hood. It was one of the special treats we ate on trips to

Israel. . . . It was creamier, fresher, and never had to be stirred from the bottom. Best of all, Israeli yogurt came in flavors like mocha, butterscotch and even chocolate. . . . I did not anticipate the degree to which the taste and texture of Austrian yogurt would invoke my memories of Israel. Walking through the dairy section of the supermarket in Salzburg, I was delighted to discover my favorite chocolate yogurt from Israel, the kind with the tuft of whipped cream on the top. . . . I was transported back to the SuperSol supermarket on Tchernischovsky Street in Tel Aviv. (207)

I lived on fresh bread, fresh fruit, spinach blintzes, dairy, and smoked fish, almost never eating meat, which was not just unpredictable in quality but also burdened with religious dogma. The Tel Aviv University dorms were set up as apartment suites, with four doubles sharing one bathroom and one "kitchen"—two burners, oven, fridge. Although my own suite-mates were not particularly Orthodox, other students' ties to keeping kosher meant trouble if meat and dairy cooked together in an oven or saucepot, and most suites stayed vegetarian to avoid the whole issue of separation and stove *kashering*. With our limited burner-top cookery options, few of us were prepared to attempt our grandmothers' holiday dishes anyway; nor did we keep many leftovers lying around, as the *jukim* (flying cockroach) problem was a modern plague. *"Juk! Juk! Juk!"* screamed my Russian suitemate, a six-foot opera student, anytime she caught sight of a winged intruder, and at the sound of her panicked contralto, the entire building would wake. But groceries had to be bought in advance for weekends, since even secular Tel Aviv shut its shops on Friday afternoon, and nothing re-opened again until Saturday night.

A peaceful Shabbat afternoon at Tel Aviv U meant sitting on the balcony of my dorm room in Binyan Bet (Building B), listening to the famous Voice of Peace radio station sustained by visionary Abie Nathan ("From somewhere in the Mediterranean, we are the Voice of Peace, *kol ha shalom*") and eating delicately frosted Hadar White Roses cookies or cracking sunflower seeds, studying, eating. The chocolate bars were slab-sized, all Elite: choco-croquant, milk, milk filled with raspberry, with orange, with hazelnut, with strawberry. When you went to the movies on Saturday night, once the buses started running again, you took a chocolate bar; the movies sold no popcorn and few snacks. Because of the heat, the chocolate softened in the dark, melted down your wrists.

I had a sheet of shelf-paper from the local Elite candy store tacked up on my wall like a political poster; the ubiquitous Elite ad looked, in Hebrew, like it spelled NIFY if you read left to right and pretended it was English.

That was dorm cuisine. On weekdays, one could also wander down to the courtyard snack bar operated by a Sephardi family whose three kids sold us *artik, borekas, garinim*. Across the street was a café called The Cage, which specialized in "shnitzel" and milkshakes. The first time I ordered a milkshake there I was puzzled to be asked, "Chocolate?" and then, after I nodded, "What flavor ice cream?" I soon found out that the chocolate factor was syrup, spread in lacelike patterns over the interior of a soda glass. The ice cream mix then filled up the glass and slowly, slowly the chocolate lace dissolved internally, sliding down the see-through sides to stud the creamy shake with bits of dark sweetness. I never tired of watching this magic trick.

Every other weekend, though, I headed to the *takana merkazeet*, the old Central Bus Station, and took off for Jerusalem or Tiberias or Eilat.

Jerusalem was forty minutes away, the bus crowded with soldiers and rabbis and schoolgirls, everyone's religious and/or political affiliation advertised by dress: uniform, skullcap, long skirt, beard, turban. A bus deposited Old City seekers at Jaffa Gate. One deep breath and then into the walls of history, the smells and sounds surging up like surf waves to soak and slap the body. Coffee, donkey, urine, incense, cardamom. *Bagele bagele bagele.* Druze ovens baking, baskets of spices, almonds, henna, mint. *Yes? You like? Come in, you are beautiful, best price.*

Any American girl out alone was fair game, sexually targeted by Jew, Arab, vendor, soldier, rabbi (yes!), everyman. Lingering anonymously, pausing to smell, taste, sample, was an exercise in eluding hands that grabbed. Bargaining in markets brought sexual propositions. One could not dine alone. I was always moving, my eyes hidden behind sunglasses. I bought food on the run: bags of Jordan almonds, Jaffa cookies, cups of fresh-squeezed juice. I traveled with a spoon, running into markets for a grapefruit or a yogurt. When I stayed at youth hostels, where food was often stolen from communal fridges, my trick was storing yogurt in the freezer. I'd have "frozen yogurt" in the morning when I left.

From my journal, at twenty:

> On bus 25 to Tel Aviv's beaches, I see signs advertise Tempo-Squash, Tropit, Burger Ranch, Sammy; on the beach lone popsicle salesmen lug coolers as they screech *Hallo, artik, limon, tut-vanil, meesh-meesh!* And the men, the men, the endless men hitting on me should I dare to buy an *artik,* soldiers calling *I see you eat ice cream. Nice ice cream you have. How you feel when you lick ice cream? You speak English? Hebrew? I can love you in any language. Come, eat your ice cream with me.*

I turned twenty-one in Israel, and it was a Friday night, the Sabbath, and everything was closed. I couldn't even get a bus to town. No matter; by then I was romantically involved with my roommate, and we made a candlelight meal in our dorm room, which had one of the best balconies in Building B. The palm tree rustled right where we draped our laundry—though on this night we probably tidied up in style. I remember standing at the tiny kitchen counter in a long brown dress, chopping tomatoes, my hair up, feeling like a woman, while my lover cut slices of a rum-soaked cake from a Tel Aviv bakery. When the restaurants opened, again, on Saturday night, we chose a little café by the beach and ordered fish. It came half-cooked, its eyes staring up at us balefully, representative of the quality and service available in restaurants at that time. You took your chances, dining out in Israel; no one knew from fancy. It was enough to be alive, and young and hungry; the nation was just thirty-four years old when I turned twenty-one.

Much has changed since then; although today, in 2011/5771, food is still the daily relief, the daily pursuit and the one permitted pleasure in this war zone. But at Bar-Ilan University, associate professor Susan Sered's research on militarism in Israeli society suggests that "Israeli girls have been found to rank highest of twenty-three European countries in dieting to lose weight. . . . By eighth grade, 10.5% of girls report dieting under the supervision of a physician, indicating that at least some of the Israeli medical establishment actively encourages the culture of dieting" (151). This shift toward Westernized ideals of a slim, nonmaternal female appearance is a sad departure from the hefty-girl magazine ads I adored in Israel in 1981; yet in at least one instance, the agenda of diet consciousness has actually united women from opposing political camps.

In her film *A Slim Peace*, director Yael Luttwak follows fourteen women brought together in a Jerusalem weight-loss clinic despite their diverging backgrounds as modern Israelis, Palestinian activists, and ultra-right-wing Orthodox settlers. How the anxiety and stress of a dysfunctional, warring society leads each to seek comfort in food is barely addressed—clearly, weight is not the real problem in their individual lives, but has become the one individual issue they do have the power and agency to change, and the one "safe" topic (controlling overeating) the women can broach in a group made up of enemy-others. The film shows us that while the weight comes off, nothing else in daily society changes: only by special dispensation are the Palestinians even allowed through degrading checkpoints into Jerusalem. (Another health issue, heavy smoking, can be understood as a small permitted pleasure in a life of forced line-waiting.) And the right-wing settlers have no intention of finding long-term rapprochement; theirs is a biblically interpreted right of occupation.

What I enquired of the young filmmaker, during a special screening at the Washington, D.C., Jewish Community Center in 2007, was whether the women in the film *used food as nationalism* during sessions at the diet clinic. Did anyone insist, "I don't care if it's fattening—this is the food staple of *my village*"? Did anyone push to have low-calorie choices that were more identifiably Arab or Ashkenazi on the idealized diet? Did the Palestinian women refuse to buy Made-in-Israel products with Hebrew lettering . . . like *Milky*? But no. In spite of the emphasis on articulating the meaning of inherited ethnic differences, and the film's food subtext, the *taste* of one's culture was not the most important thing; having—and perpetuating—a culture, whether it pushed out or threatened another's destiny, was.

The one item everyone ate in common was locally grown olives. And I thought of the ancient symbol of the olive branch, the vineyard as peace symbol.

That December I bought Palestinian olive oil and *zatar* from a women's cooperative, and used it to fry my latkes, during Chanukah; in my own kitchen, such a ritual site of separation, for Jews who keep kosher and Arabs eating *halal,* I could create an uncontested border-crossing, a culinary détente.

Food is pleasure, and so my memories of Israel retain liminal associations of eating, respites from warfare and violence. Old flavors fill my mouth whenever someone asks if I have been to Israel, if I once broke bread there. In these times, when the same "family friendly" catalog advertising *darling chocolate plagues* also sells Israel Defense Forces jewelry made out of nonlive steel bullets (right next to silver birds of peace!), it is difficult to write of the past in a neutral, food-sensory way. I have to drive to Koshermart in Silver Spring to find a cup of *Milky*, listening to the Voice of Peace on old cassette tapes from '81.

SOURCES

Ruth A. Abusch-Magder, "Making Love on the Deutsche Bahn," in *Joining the Sisterhood: Young Jewish Women Write Their Lives,* ed. Tobin Belzer and Julie Pelc. New York: SUNY, 2003. Print.

Harvard Student Agencies, *Let's Go Europe 1982.* New York: St. Martin's, 1982. Print.

Samuel C. Heilman, *Sliding to the Right.* Berkeley: U of California P, 2006. Print.

Susan Sered, *What Makes Women Sick?* Lebanon, NH: Brandeis UP/UPNE, 2000. Print.

Richard Sterling, *The Fearless Diner.* San Francisco: Travelers' Tales, 1998. Print.

THE CULTURE OF SELF AND SPIRIT

"You have looked into the eyes / of your creature self . . ."

— Stanley Kunitz (1905–), *King of the River*, 1971

Connections Betty Jo Goddard

Palo del Muerte Simmons B. Buntin

Betty Jo Goddard has traveled a packed road since her birth in Windsor, Illinois. While on that road, she acquired a BS from Illinois State and an MA from the University of Colorado. After twenty-five years of teaching intermediate-aged students in Illinois, Colorado, and Alaska, she retired in 1983 and now lives with three huskies on an Alaskan ridge-top in a house powered by solar panels and a wind generator. She writes to inquire and for fun, insight, and a chance to share. Goddard has published fiction and nonfiction in many publications, including *Dog and Kennel, Grit,* and *Writers' Journal,* and her stories have been heavily anthologized. She is winner of the Kenai Peninsula Writer's Contest in both fiction and nonfiction, and her poetry placed first in *Writers' Journal* 2010 poetry contest. Her books include *If You Can't Train Them, Love Them: The Dogs in My Life* (2007).

Connections

Betty Jo Goddard

Recently I read an article suggesting that friendship leads to a longer life. According to the article, one ten-year study showed that while the study was conducted, older people with a large circle of friends were 22 percent less likely to die. The article cited other studies that indicated friendship had a bigger impact on our psychological well-being than family relationships; that for men, only smoking was a greater risk factor than lack of social support; and—most intriguing to me—that strong social ties could promote *brain health* as we age (Pope).

Well, gosh sakes, I thought. And here I believed I could live a happy, healthy life with my own good company. I, who search for ways to coax my brain into firing me with the fervor of youth, got up from my computer and looked down on mooncast shadows in the uninhabited valley below and considered my lifestyle.

I love my home up here at the end of the road. It was I who had the road put in, a utilitarian choice made to meet contractors' requirements, not to make access easy for others. One friend, who used that very road to visit my ridge-top home (and me, too, I suppose), hinted that I was a hermit living way up at the end of nowhere.

"Well," I told her, "I like people, but just look." I waved at my million-dollar view. "I love being surrounded by nature. I love privacy to do as I wish without fear of offending, and I love freedom from a lot of social obligations."

Yes, freedom: I treasure it. I could write a piece about freedom and safety in separation, but I won't stray to alluring byroads. This piece is about friendship and connections. Do I need them in order to be happy and healthy?

If I try to answer that, I run into a trap. That trap is the word *need*.

I think of friendships I've had. When I was in high school, I walked the social fringes, matter-of-factly accepting my wall-flower status. It wasn't until college that I knew the thrill of my first kiss—which didn't thrill me at all. Norman's attempt to initiate me into French kissing felt slimy and unsanitary.

I preferred chess, table tennis, and long evening walks with Dan. But alas, Dan was two years younger than I; the possi-bility of dating an older woman never entered his head. When he told me he was taking a girl from his own class to an end-of-the-year social event, I shrugged and stalked off. Dan ran after me calling, "Bets, Bets, what's wrong?"

"Nothing," I said. I think I yelled it. Then I rushed from connection to seek privacy.

So my college years slipped by without shared hopes, without shared angst, without shared lacerations. I had periph-eral friends, but no heart-to-heart confidants. Even in later adulthood, I hid my deepest feelings. With friends, I listened, told a few stories, occasionally reflected. Mostly our sharings were outer-directed—as a teenager, Cub ball games; later, with my women friends, men. Our sharing was speculative—would they or wouldn't they?—but not deeply personal.

New enterprises pulled. I ranged further. Old friendships faded.

Was it happenstance or grace? My wanderings led me to friends who offered grist for my mind. Verbal sparring sent brain wheels spinning, nudged me to new ways of looking at behavior (mine and others'), and dared me to consider the effi-cacy of those ways. I quivered with mental stimulation and glowed in heart stimulation. These friendships broadened my perspectives, walked with me in tough situations, and stretched me with aggravation and abrasions. They provided bubbling petri dishes where I floundered and grew. Yes, the article I read was right: They fed my brain health.

But do I *need* friendships for better health? My current ridge-top home isn't the first place I've lived at "the end of nowhere," as my friend termed it. When I was in my thirties, I fixed up a ten-by-twenty-foot prove-up shack so it was livable. (When people staked property in Alaska, they were required to make improvements on the land they staked. This was called "proving up" on the land.) For my first two years there, I *walked* to my home; no road led there. As I carried food or drinking water along a hemlock-lined path to my little cabin, my heart expanded. I embraced the path, the forest, the glowing ridge beyond. No neighbors bordered the trail to jolt my serenity. Not a single one. This, I thought, is mine, all mine.

I think that same thought now, as I stand at a window in my ridge-top home and take in glaciers, volcanoes, and silent, undemanding wilderness. Only among swarms of people have I felt lonely. I grew up in a large family teeming with clatter, orders, disorder. I longed for space—even a little corner—where I could be by myself, free of demand. Now I revel in that space, that freedom, that aloneness. I love the still air clear of the rush and clatter of commerce—and, yes, of close neighbors. Have I sacrificed something healthy: connections with others?

That word *need* comes up again. I'm not "needy," I think. I don't have to be with others in order to feel good. And connections still abound. I offer six examples:

1. I first came to my ridge-top lot in 1993, cut alders, walked the land, and marveled at the thought of living here—an incipient connection. After I moved here in 1995, I worked to mold the space to my own liking. The incipient connection grew, tickled my pride, made itself known. When my mother was still alive, every couple of years I drove back to Illinois, savoring varied landscapes, soaking up their flavors, feeling their offerings. But here on my ridge-top, the landscape is special: It carries *my* stamp. Territorial inclinations crop up to deepen the connection I feel to this spot—*my* spot—overlooking nature's grand reach.

2. I remember my first car—a '54 Chevy I bought from a Fuller Brush salesman. I named it Chester and took good care of it. When the call of the wild and a teaching job pulled me to Alaska in 1963, I bought a new Chevy to brave the Alaska Highway and left Chester in a Chevrolet lot with his hood hanging down and his tailpipe between his legs. I held an affinity with this car—a ready servant that protected me from the elements when I traveled and took me where I wanted to go without complaint. I hated to abandon a loyal friend with whom I felt a strong connection. I felt like crying.

3. After I retired from teaching, I busied myself with other ventures—exploring, learning, testing friendships. When, in 1993, I came to my ridge-top property, built a road and a house, put in a garden, and molded the place to my liking, I felt happy. But, something was missing: My heart didn't stretch with fondness as it had when I taught. To squirt love juice into my life, I acquired a dog and named him Peter. That Peter did it: My heart stretched. I laughed, petted, loved, then grieved when Peter died. Now, in Peter's place, I have three dogs—Peggy, Perry, and Patty: connection in triplicate.

4. As I walk a dog or two the mile and a half to my mailbox, I encounter others who have moved up here. We talk. No intimacy forms, but casual friendships do and a sense of community grows: neighborhood connections.

5. Not far from here, out at the end of a spit stretching into a glacier-fed bay, the first Kachemak Bay Writer's Conference sprang to life. I enrolled and met people who invited me to join their writing group. I accepted. Every two weeks we meet, read, critique, and eat goodies together. My sphere of connections enlarged.

6. Technology offers new connections. I don't Twitter, I don't tweet, I don't bother with MySpace or Facebook. I don't own an iPod or an iPad or an iPhone. But now I do have a phone, connected to the outer world by a cord. I do have an iMac. I do have email. These speed communications free me from scratching addresses on envelopes, open quick avenues for research, and bring me news from the outer world.

Such connections, I could tell my friend, are available even to "hermits" living on a ridge-top at the end of nowhere. Are they needed? No. But they enrich my life. My life is full of potential connections. All I have to do is muster them, choose them, feel them, value them.

Recently I lost my feeling of connection: When I tried to turn on my computer, no light came on, no array of icons sprang forth to greet me, no messages filled my email inbox. I was *not* serene. Desperate, I hauled my heretofore-loyal iMac to a technician in Homer. For three days, a void emptied my world. I chafed at emails I couldn't access, at responses I couldn't make. I, the so-called hermit, felt disconnected.

I think of the small cabin where I lived for four years with no road reaching me, no phone, no close neighbors. Back then, I embraced my world without phone, Internet, or email, and felt at one with life. I smile when I realize how the email-habit has snared me—demanding, insistent, time-consuming. Connection, I see, is a state of mind. When my computer returned, ready and eager, I once again felt connected to the rest of the world.

Someone once asked me if using modern technology's offerings was a sell-out or a perk. For me, having electricity (albeit via solar panels and wind generators), indoor plumbing, and expedient means of communication are definitely perks. I'm still embraced by both the serenity and the tempestuousness of sparsely-peopled nature. I receive only a half dozen or so calls a week on my land line. Those I can answer or not as I choose. So silence still rests my ears and soothes my mind. I savor my up, out, and away life, but don't insist on doing things the way my grandparents did. If technology will save me time to do more of what I really want to do, I welcome it into my home.

Along my seventy-eight-year journey, I perceived a greater connection emerging—*a connection with myself and my own knowing.* Others hinted, or pointedly told me how I should behave, what kind of person I should be, what I should believe, what paths I should take—even how I should dress. I listened. My mind resonated with much I heard; much of it I questioned. Social connections tugged me this way and that. How I worried what others would think. Torn, I edged my way on bypaths, not wanting to disappoint good, well-meaning people by walking my own path, not theirs.

But those connections jabbed me awake. And I am

grateful—*am I ever*—for those connections goaded me to hearken to inner promptings and to heed whispers of mysterious forces unnoted by physical senses—forces that guide me to choose paths that resonate with my deepest sense of truth, so that more and more, I know my own true self. May I never betray that connection, for I do think *that* connection, more than any other, is what will keep me healthy and whole.

SOURCE

Tara Parker Pope, "What Are Friends For? A Longer Life." *New York Times*, 20 April 2009: n. pg. Web. 21 April 2009.

Simmons B. Buntin is the youngest son of a Swedish immigrant who married an American after living, as a young adult, in Italy and Rhodesia (now Zimbabwe), as well as in Sweden. Buntin lives with his wife and two daughters in the Sonoran desert of southern Arizona. He and his family often travel across the border into Mexico, where he has been greatly influenced by the mix of indigenous and Catholic beliefs in a landscape rich in cultural and ecological diversity. He is the author of two poetry books, *Bloom* (2010) and *Riverfall* (2005), and his essays and poetry have been published in such journals as *Orion, North American Review, Kyoto Journal,* and in the University of Utah's *Wildbranch* anthology on nature, environmental, and place-based writing (2010). He is editor of the award-winning online journal *Terrain.org,* which focuses on the natural and built environments.

Palo del Muerte

Simmons B. Buntin

Here, we, where the white wood stands,
together we meet,
together we will talk about this animal.

— from an untitled Yaqui deer song
    by Don Jesús Yoilo'i

1.

This animal that is a god, or God. This god that is ever-present, or ever-distant. This god that is in all things created—the wilderness, the moon and sun, the pulsing galaxies beyond—or the god that is the Genesis and the Exodus, no longer a god. This god that is a universe, at once in and of everything, or the god that is a machine, our machine, an enterprise of self-replicating technology, the temple and its congregation of inventors. This god in the indigo eyes of my daughters, or the god of plague and terror and genocide. This god of indifference.

2.

The dark shape of an eagle moves across the stretched-glass sky, high enough to leave a vapor trail, then orbits back toward earth. The earth is the rich desert of northwest Mexico, below the granite hills of Hermosillo, Sonora. Though not wealthy in the context of industry or market, the landscape here offers a gilded mix of plants, a lush portfolio of flowers and trees and succulents. The organ pipe cactus, for instance, grows in gray-green columns, often jointed, two dozen arms rising twenty feet or more. During summer nights, blooms appear at their tips: gold-centered flowers that share their dividends with bats, doves, and more. But Sonoran plants are sharp and, like the animals, sometimes poisonous. They are weary and withdraw in the heat of the day. And they are enigmatic, able to withstand six-month summers—dormant, as if dying or already dead.

On the thornscrub plains that slide into the Sea of Cortés, there is one such mysterious plant: *palo del muerte*. Stick of the dead; tree morning glory. For much of the year the silvery tree is leafless, its branches shining like white tributaries against the azure sky, the trunk a lit stream among cardón and mesquite. As the midsummer rains sweep across Sonora, the *palo del muerte* explodes into an emerald plume of leaves that drop— sensitive to the waning light, the cooling night—just four months later. Over the mild winter, clusters of white flowers bloom at the ends of branches. The flowers last longer than the leaves, opening in the morning so that each tree sparkles like a constellation, as if the whole theater of the sky awoke in the humble branches of a tree. It must take all day for the ruby-centered stars to find their way back, visited in the meantime by hawkmoths and hummingbirds. And when they fall, the deer eat them, stealing the light before noon, so that the astronomers are right: everything, ultimately, comes from the stars—a brilliance that fills us all.

3.

As a boy, a recurring vision held me before I slept. In a trance of half-slumber, I lifted from my bed, rose into the night, and glided beyond the blue sphere of the earth. The body leaving the body, I remained a boy's form—my own pale arms and legs—but had no weight. Each evening I prepared myself by slowing my breath, fixing my eyes behind dull lids, willing my spirit's separation. Skin tingled as energy pulsed, as muscles tightened and then released. Like a geyser breaking from the ground, my spirit erupted as the body subsided, deflated, perhaps never existing at all.

Absent of time and distance, I drifted through an astral world until finding a silver channel, a vast pane of light that divided the night like a crucifix into quadrants. Below the horizon, the sky loomed dark and barren. But above the arms of the cross, a dusky window brightened into day on my approach. I floated over the threshold and into a vast wilderness heavy with water and life, then landed in a massive tree, moss draping, vines as thick as pythons. The primeval jungle was nearly unbearable in its vibrancy—the mad songs of birds and frogs, deer leaping among the fronds, jaguars racing, the plants themselves riotous in their green joy.

For many years I associated those visions with my spirit, and in that sense they became my true identity just as they became a drug, a nightly elixir that numbed me to the chaos of this world and delivered me to the next, if only briefly. But what was this place, and how did I find it night after night, exhausted to dreamless sleep upon my return? Was it heaven or the garden before the fall? Where was my family then and yet to come?

4.

An animal tunnels beneath the lime-white roots of a young *palo del muerte*, the same roots once eaten by the Yaqui of central Sonora. It may be centipede or millipede, wood rat or gopher snake. The roots are thick and bulbous, like sweet potatoes, and the meat soft, like balsa. Wild burros and livestock graze its argent bark during drought. Sometimes they eat the entire trunk and the white tree falls—a stream run dry, a constellation inked out.

I am troubled by my own fall and uncertainty of beliefs and experiences: the passing of faith as my wife Billie and I raise our young daughters in a secular home. How do parents of differing beliefs teach their children to, if not have faith, then at least have hope?

Billie once believed that God created the world and then drifted away. When she was five, her single mother dropped her off at church every Sunday before heading to work. Billie attended by herself, of her own will, curious in the faith and community and convinced, then, in a benevolent God. Yet by the time she was twelve, she stopped attending services because she no longer believed. Her mother worked multiple jobs, often late into the night. At the edge of poverty, Billie could not understand how a god could allow her family and indeed most of the world to "struggle so endlessly." An atheist most of her life, she now believes that God and religion simply do not matter. "What matters," she says, "is being a good person."

5.

A mourning dove calls from a single desert tree: *coo-wah coo coo coo,* the soft echo of emptiness. The tree, an acacia, leans out of the dry lawn of Whitmore Elementary School, where in fourth grade my leg broke. Playing a pick-up game of football, I was tackled from behind. I woke paralyzed, it seemed, except my head, which swayed back and forth beneath the glaring sky, the pain extreme but empty, building and releasing, breaking in uneven waves from the snapped femur that bulged like the enflamed bud of a desert lily. There was no red blossom; the bone had not torn my flesh. A crowd of students gathered, the teachers huddled, and paramedics rushed in. My mother appeared. A visage of white-blue moon stained the afternoon, then disappeared behind the shape of a man who sliced my tan corduroys to reveal the white bulb of the broken bone just beneath my skin, glorious and sickening.

I woke hours later at Tucson Medical Center, my left leg lifted in traction, the swelling gone but a pin drilled into my fibula, below my kneecap, then tied to a system of pullies that kept the two halves of my femur in place. In the bed next to me, a Mexican boy named Jesús heard my groaning as I heard his. Jesus? I had never known the name of Christ used for another person.

After traction and the four-hour surgery that placed me in a hard, spread-eagle cast; after the nurses demonstrated how to bathe me and turn me; and after the wild ambulance ride where the driver thought a little excitement might do me good, I came home. After that, I saw the angel.

I heard him first, in the hallway outside my bedroom, where the door was open. Calling, I thought it was my sister, but there was no reply. In a hooded cloak the color of Manila paper, the figure moved past the doorframe, gliding through the hallway and soon out of sight. His face was hidden and he didn't look my way, but he had the height and, if possible to tell beneath the muted outline of the cloak, the build of a man. I should have been scared or otherwise paralyzed, but was neither. It is not quite right to say there was a sudden calm—a warm blanket or the sweet scent of citrus—yet a sense of the serene overcame me, so I didn't tell my mother until the evening.

"Your guardian angel," she said, unworried, full of a faith akin to spirituality more than religion. Though not a Christian, nor a member of any organized religion, my silver-haired mother held a strong belief in the supernatural, in the presence of her own psychic senses as much as a "higher power" she called God. Years later, when I was a student at a parochial high school, when I struggled with the idea of a singular, Christian God, she had sensible answers of no doctrine other than her own. "God wears many masks," she said, "and He uses those masks, those religions, to reach people of different faiths." Heretical from a Christian point of view, but acceptable from her global perspective. "Each is holy in his own belief" was her mantra, an eloquent outlook especially from a woman who grew up Lutheran, in Sweden, under the cloak of state religion.

My guardian angel? St. Jerome, the ecclesiastical wanderer who died in Bethlehem in 420 C.E., read many passages of the Bible to mean that each person has a guardian angel to lead him or her to the kingdom of heaven. "How great the dignity of the soul, since each one has from his birth an angel commissioned to guard it," he wrote. Sentenced to a full body cast, did I now need a guardian angel? Maybe, though my struggles were greater in the coming months, during rehabilitation, as I learned how to bend my knee, how to walk again.

The most difficult days, however, came several years later, when like my mother I found myself alternately depressed or manic, sad or ecstatic, a boy sometimes suicidal—the product, we hoped, of the chemical imbalances of adolescence. That may explain the timing of the second and final sighting. At our next Tucson home, not far from the adobe ruins of Fort Lowell and along the banks of a wide arroyo, I entered the house to see the angel, rising. His unwinged back moving from me, the figure climbed the stairs and turned at the landing to enter my room. I followed, finding the room bright with morning light yet otherwise vacant.

6.

For much of my life, I have considered myself spiritual, though not religious. The difference has less to do with etymology than architecture. The word *spiritual*—pertaining to the spirit or soul—derives from the Latin word *spiritus*, meaning "breath." The origin of *religious*—having or showing belief in and reverence for God or a deity—is less clear. Though also Latin, its source could be *relegere*, "to read again"; or *religore*, "to bind fast," as in a bond between humans and the gods; or even *religiens*, "careful," the opposite of *negligens*.

Religion classes at parochial schools and conversations with pious parents cast religion as a high-walled, unwavering bastion—a monolith where decisions and judgments were handed down from on high, where despite the teachings of love and forgiveness, the dogma was accusatory and full of wrath. Ornate ceremonies fit my view of this citadel; not a part of my early youth, they were foreign and uncomfortable. I could not stand the cold vulnerability.

Then as now, spirituality represented freedom in unordained faith—an integral though indefinable sustenance from a power beyond the self, beyond the world, yet wholly connected. Religion, on the other hand, continued to mean faith engineered from rites and observances; doctrine and practices set and largely unalterable.

There was a time, however, when I was "saved," when I fully accepted Jesus Christ as the son of God, my personal savior. I preached to my friends and mother and nearly drove them mad. Only months into freshman classes at St. John Lutheran High in Ocala, Florida, the change was swift—and necessary. A naïve (though sarcastic) boy in the footsteps of my older, partying sister, I drank alcohol every weekend and envied her drug-taking, not yet aware of the effects on her body and spirit. I cheated on tests, didn't care if I lied, hung around with the proverbial wrong crowd.

After my conversion—a simple moment when I lingered

alone after class one autumn day, a moment when my new exposure to Lutheran teachings suddenly dissolved the walls so that acceptance flowered from within, as it must—I stopped drinking and cheating. And though my sarcasm remained (it was, after all, the language of youth) I strived to follow the Scriptures, to love and be loved, and spread the word. Those were enlightened days, but they didn't last. Only weeks later, I slid out of the Christian faith, deciding Jesus was a prophet, certainly, but not the son of God.

Why the sudden departure? For years I blamed it on the hypocrisy so rampant at school and, it seemed clear, throughout the Christian faith. But that was only a symptom. Better to say: It didn't stick. In the end, I could never subscribe to the idea of original sin, that infants are born in sin, spiritually if not morally cursed, and only through baptism could find sanctity.

What of the millions of others, in different religions and otherwise, who are never baptized? What of my own children? Are they condemned to a fiery afterlife? "Yes," according to the Southern Baptist who drove me to school after my sister fled to Los Angeles. "They are going to Hell, which is why our life's work is to save their souls." She undertook Bible study while steering the old Buick, eyes scanning the primer more often than the road, scaring the hell out of me and perhaps taking heaven with it.

What remained after my falling out was the desire to be lawful, and more important to be "good," a concept derived in part from the teachings of the New Testament—love one another, practice forgiveness—and in larger part from the tolerance and compassion of my mother, the steady influence in my spiritual progression even as she promoted my enrollment in parochial schools for the quality of their biased education. I didn't drink again until I turned twenty-one, studied instead of cheated, worked hard at being friendly. Other beliefs crept in, too. I adopted my mother's polyreligious doctrine—the holiness in each of our faiths, so long as no one is hurt—but didn't dwell on the details. That openness allowed me to create my own belief system, one without ritual or history but strong in purpose.

The Dharmic idea of karma, in this life and the next, took hold. Unlike the threat of eternal damnation or immediate retribution, I adopted the idea of positive reinforcement—that good deeds, while not individually rewarded, both define and direct us. Cause and effect; a seemingly scientific formula with cosmic results. And like my mother and those of Hindu and other faiths, I believed in reincarnation, assuming that after we die, our souls pass to a sort of heavenly holding tank, a lovely, gardenlike wilderness full of friends and family who also have died (an echo of us always remains in that place, I supposed), before evolving into a body capable of higher spiritual thought; until eventually becoming not just a part of God—"We are individual drops of water in the ocean of God," another of my mother's sayings—but actually becoming God. That is the purpose of life, I believed: to evolve spiritually.

"I always knew there were people like you," said a college sophomore after I told her my thoughts on reincarnation, "but I never thought I'd actually meet one." From a small Alabama town with a quaint Baptist church and a sheltered faith in the literal Word, she was taken aback, and likely appalled, because she never returned my calls after our first date.

Where is God now? I wondered. Never believing that God simply vanished after creating the earth, the solar system, or the universe, I saw holiness all around me, yet only in our natural places—the swift springs at the source of a subtropical river, for example, or the airy halls of the longleaf pine forest just outside my door. The question became: *What is God?* The answer was logical, inasmuch as logic plays a role in any spiritual belief: God is nature and nature is God. I began to think of myself as a druid—not a cleric of nature spirits, but a worshipper of nature in the church of bluejack oak, the cathedral of old-growth pines. I was a member of the congregation of the great outdoors.

What, then, of humans? Are people a part of nature, and therefore a part of God? My mother thought so, believing strongly in interconnectedness, the indecipherable linkages between people and the universe—whether people choose to recognize them or not. Yet I saw people as separate. Civilization and technology were, if not antithetical to nature, then artificial. Constructed. What else could explain deforestation, strip mining, damming the wild rivers? War and famine. Why would God destroy God?

Looking back, I see the immediate conflict—people *apart*

from nature, and, therefore, apart from God, yet whose purpose in life was to *evolve into* God. The conflict has not resolved, though an easy bridge is indigenous cultures. Even large environmental organizations like the World Wildlife Fund now recognize that wildlands are most successfully preserved not absent of native peoples, but because of them. They are an intrinsic part of their natural habitats. Another bridge is children, whose innocence and curiosity link them to nature so that natural habitats become an integral part of who they are. At what point, though, is the linkage lost, and why?

7.

The coyote will not eat crushed mesquite beans from my hand, though my daughters and I coax the wary canine from beneath a knot of mesquites outside our Tucson home. Do my children see God in his umber eyes, in the heavy-branched native trees, in the Rincon Mountains, vermilion in the coming dusk? We've had conversations about religion—Juliet's best friend is Mormon, and asks my younger daughter about her relationship with Jesus almost daily, though her parents are not evangelical and have never approached us about their faith—but not *the* conversation, the "Does God exist?" query. If prompted, I might default to my answer about the tooth fairy and Santa Claus, who my six- and nine-year-old daughters still believe in: They are real so long as you believe in them. But I do not classify God with the tooth fairy or Easter bunny or Santa Claus. Even as I struggle with my own faith, I favor a deist approach—that there is a central spiritual force in our world and the worlds beyond that operates on and above science and reason; that the force, the unending energy, binds us to place; that, after all, "each is holy in his own belief." How, otherwise, can we respect indigenous beliefs?

The Yaqui believe in a dual world, a universe of parallels—this desert landscape and a "mythic, primeval place called . . . *sea ania*, flower world," say Larry Evers and Felipe S. Molina in *Yaqui Deer Songs: Maso Bwikam*. The worlds are bridged by the deer dancer and the men who, in support of this sacred performance, sing the deer songs. The songs themselves, write Evers and Molina, "tell a continuing story of life and death in the wilderness world of the Sonoran desert." And they bring forth the voice of *saila maso*, the deer who is exalted among all others in the flower world, in the afterlife, to the east.

The *palo del muerte* represents *sea ania*, the flower world, at least to me, a man who is not Yaqui, whose knowledge of Yaqui ceremony and beliefs is limited, and who has rarely seen the tree. It's a dangerous comparison, though, because it comes without authority, a kind of socioreligious anthropomorphism. Yet it's a metaphor that works: the clustered flowers that shine as if from another world, and the deer that eat them after they fall. The branches like silver antlers, and the resurgence of leaves and life with the summer rains. The tree is not a portal, but a symbol—an allegory for my own otherworldly pursuit. God as nature, nature as God: the ancient wilderness here and beyond.

If nature is God, then God is inherently neutral—neither good nor evil. Yet, like Billie, I strive to be an involved, inspirational, and encouraging parent and community member, to treat others with fairness, to use compassion at all times. How to graft the disparate branches? While I agree that nature cannot intrinsically favor good or evil—even as humans seem to exhibit the full spectrum—I must believe in the overall good of self, the possibilities of good in the world, if I want to seed hope in my daughters. And hope is the essential seed. I am not certain of hope's relationship to spiritual evolution; maybe they are the same. Maybe hope is the vine that climbs beyond the flower-tipped branches.

8.

This animal beneath the white tree is me, and the trail is of my making. Billie and I have followed our own paths—she without parental guidance, I with insight from my mother. There seems to be a difference. Without her mother or father raising her in faith—religious or otherwise—Billie has none. No faith, that is, in a force or transcendent spirit beyond the self, though it's clear—as a teacher and idealist—she has faith in herself, in education, in family and community. "Be good," she says. It's the *being* that counts, not the tallying of deeds to be scrutinized at a pearly gate.

Yet my visions as a child—the strangely tangible faith I sometimes miss, sometimes decline—lead me to believe that even when we do not seek it, even when our parents and the wider community do not immerse us in it, spirituality has a way of finding each of us. Grace seeks us as much as we seek grace.

Perhaps, then, matters of faith may be learned but not actively taught. Perhaps by our actions and conversations alone, which are more than mere indifference, our children also find their own way, a path that encourages discovery through the world around us—the lofty flight of eagle and low song of dove, the skittish lope of coyote and quick curve of centipede. And perhaps curiosity—its own kind of *sea ania,* the flower world both within and beyond—is enough.

When we first saw the *palo del muerte* on the bajadas below Hermosillo, my daughters knew it wasn't dead because, against the low winter sun, the flowers flared. "Like an angel," said Juliet, who traced the tree's outline against the tinted glass of our car. "Like an angel," I echoed, considering the soul's guardian—an angel, an illusion, the deep-seeded self?—as we journey through this life and the next.

QUESTIONS FOR DISCUSSION

Intercultural Considerations

Intercultural Connections

Quotation Exploration

INTERCULTURAL CONSIDERATIONS

If Grandmother Had Married a Peasant

1. In the opening paragraph, Lovett refers to herself as being "Mao's poster child." Who is Mao, and what tone does this set for the rest of the essay?

2. Some of us have grown up hearing that we should finish all the food on our plates because there are "starving children in China." Does it surprise you to hear Lovett's mother use this same tactic on p. 2?

3. In many ways, this essay is one large What If? question. What is Lovett imagining throughout, and how does volunteering as a peasant on p. 4 answer her question?

4. What conclusions does Lovett come to about being Chinese American? What have you learned about China that you didn't know before reading this essay?

5. NET assignment: Go to Google Images and search for "Chinese Peasants." What images come up, and how do the images compare to Lovett's descriptions?

Fragments: Finding Center

1. Have you heard the term *Third Culture Kid* before? Do you know anyone who may be considered a Third Culture Kid? If so, do Stoner's experiences parallel theirs (or yours, if you are a TCK)?

2. Though somewhat unflattering, "army brat" is another label used to describe children whose military parents are constantly on the move, not just from state to state, but from country to country. What challenges come from constant uprooting? What benefits might there be?

3. Have you met someone like Stoner who has a completely different cultural background than you do? If so, what was your reaction? Why do you think she is uncomfortable in both "Takes" on pp. 13–14? Or when eating french fries?

4. Stoner relays how television is a culture in itself. Have you ever felt left out of a group because you didn't understand a cultural reference? Did you let on that you were confused, or did you play along? If the group found out, what was their reaction?

5. NET assignment: Do research on Third Culture Kids (also TCK, 3CK). Watch the trailer for *Les Passagers: a TCK story* at tckacademy.com/tckfilm/. Where did the term come from? Who are these kids, and what are their concerns? How might you reach out to them and make them feel more at home?

Giiwe: go home

1. The essay begins with a fire, set by an arsonist. What is the target? What does Stark's reaction to this criminal act tell you about her past? What does this act of arson tell you about U.S. culture?

2. Stark's description of the borderland settlement between Canada and North Dakota is a compelling indictment of the founding of one settlement within the United States. Do you agree with her history and her theory of the mixed-bloods?

3. In Utah, Stark and her partner become wary when approached by "two cowboys." Why? Do you think they are overreacting and guilty of prejudice themselves? Have you ever felt fearful of another group based on appearance or history?

4. Stark clearly feels most comfortable in the landscape she grew up in, despite the violence. How strong is the lure of childhood environment to you? Have you moved away from where you were born and raised? Do you feel at "home" with your surroundings and yourself? And what is "home" to you?

5. NET assignment: Stark is in a position many mixed-bloods find themselves in—unable to feel a part of one community. Her friends feel she has a right to be part of the Native American community, but some tribes are beginning to draw the lines more firmly between belonging and being an outsider. Do some research on this part of current tribal law to discover the arguments for and against tribal membership. After exploring both sides, which opinion do you agree with, and why?

Bufferhood: An Autoethnography

1. Sartwell's essay begins with a short email from her mother, revealing that she is typing directly on the computer for the first time. This begins an exchange with both her mother and her grandfather on family history. In the past, history was recorded first through oral stories, which had to be

memorized, then through writing on paper, which eventually degrades. Has the Internet changed how people are connected and recording their histories? What long-term effect might this function of the Internet have on the future and on family connections?

2. Sartwell's great-grandfather got into an altercation with an immigration officer over the pronunciation and spelling of his last name. What was the result of this altercation? Was your own family name changed at any point in history? If so, why? And have you thought of changing it back?

3. What is beautifully rendered in these letters is the ephemeral quality of memory. Can we trust that we know our family history implicitly, if human memory is flawed? And if this is a problem within the microcosm of the family, what does this say about society as a whole?

4. Sartwell discusses the dilemma of not feeling either white or Jewish, of being a "buffer" zone, and the issue of whiteness no longer referring just to skin color. Do you sympathize with her in any way? Do you agree with her theory on whiteness and the Jews as being a buffer between blacks and whites? And what does the noun "white" mean to you?

5. NET assignment: Go to an ancestry site online and start your own genealogy chart, or do research and add more to a chart that a family member may already have started. Do any surprises pop up? If so, how do the surprises make you feel?

Valentine and This Difficult World

1. Klebenov Jacobs explores in depth her family history. What is her purpose? What stereotypes do her relatives fall into? Who imagines those stereotypes?

2. Klebenov Jacobs asks a very loaded question: Is my grandmother anti-Semitic? Do you agree with her eventual answer? Why or why not?

3. Condensed historical facts are given to measure the grandmother's life. How do these facts support the view "Granny" has? Do you think they justify her outlook?

4. After reading the personal, historical letters, how does the final letter at the end of the essay come across to you? Why do you think the author placed it in this position?

5. NET assignment: Look up the term "WASP" (White

Anglo-Saxon Protestant). How does this group fit into U.S. or European history? What about the culture has improved or hurt society? If you have this background, how does your family feel about outsiders?

Reflecting on Dragons and Angels

1. Bannwart titles her essay "Reflecting on Dragons and Angels." How does it relate to her recollection? What meaning can you infer from it?

2. Does this essay's point of view by a German child about the "end" of World War II surprise you in any way? Why or why not?

3. For many U.S. students, the Iraq War has been the backdrop of their childhood. How does it differ from actually being in the country of occupation and battle? How is it similar?

4. What does it mean to be a "winner" in your culture? Or a loser? Are the labels fair, in your estimation? And what do the meanings reflect about each culture?

5. NET assignment: Look up "Volksempfänger" and "World War II people's radio," and research its history and purpose. Why do you think the Freedom of Speech Act is such an important law in the United States?

Tongue-Tied

1. Women in Iraq have a different role in society than they do in the United States. What in this essay can you find that points to Iraqi gender attitudes?

2. What role does the photo play in reconnecting Hayes-Raitt with Nebras? Why is the fact that it's a photo seem so important to the child?

3. In December 2011, U.S. President Barack Obama withdrew all troops from Iraq after an eight-year occupation. What role did the United States play in supporting or destroying Iraqi culture during the war? What happened to Iraq's museums? To its government?

4. NET assignment: Do research into the legality of begging and the different cultural attitudes toward it. What might these attitudes say about each culture that holds them?

Tightrope Across the Abyss

1. "Tightrope" centers on a documentary. What is the subject of the film, and how is it a reflection of Bannwart's own crisis of identity?

2. Are you surprised at the deep guilt and trauma that relations of German Nazis struggle with? Do you believe their guilt is justified? Why or why not?

3. On p. 64, Ruth says, "A lot of Jewish survivors would not agree with me, meeting a Nazi descendent." Do you agree, based on your own cultural upbringing? Why or why not?

4. Bannwart repeatedly theorizes that she is witnessing "a female approach to making peace." Consider this statement, and discuss whether or not you feel men and women have different cultural approaches to making peace, and whether or not countries have different approaches. If so, how does this encounter cross over cultural boundaries?

5. NET assignment: Do some research on the film *Bloodlines* (at bloodlinesfilm.com) and on Ruth Rich's Holocaust paintings. If you can't find any of Rich's works, look for other artists' renderings. What more can you discover on the impact this war has had on these two women's lives, or on the lives of other artists you explored?

A Dash of Pepper in the Snow

1. Autman relays many instances of racist behavior. What are they? Have you experienced racial or gender stereotyping? If so, how can you relate to Autman? If not, do you feel his stories are justified, or is he overreacting?

2. On pp. 83–85, Autman both excoriates and defends Mormons. How can he hold two differing opinions of one group?

3. Autman sets up the reader, so to speak. We think we are reading an essay entirely about his negative feelings toward the racist remarks and attitudes he encounters. Then, just at the end, he does an abrupt about-face. What does his final experience reveal? How does this affect your overall view of his essay?

4. NET assignment: Look into Mormon history. How and why did the Mormons settle in Utah? Within the context of this essay, does the reason surprise you?

"Miss Otis Regrets"

1. This essay delves into a topic most people have difficulty discussing. As you read Parker's essay, did you relate to her in any way? If not, did her honesty help you to think of racial discomfort in another light? What feelings did it evoke?

2. Does knowing the ethnic background of the author and her husband inform your reading in any way? If so, how?

3. Parker chooses to believe in her tragic version of the song, despite the research that appears to prove Cole Porter's intentions were otherwise. Given the period when Porter was writing (lynching still occurring), what version do you believe, and why? Could Parker be right? Why or why not?

4. Parker speaks for many about the discomfort of racial relations. What solutions can you offer to people like her and to those she is uncomfortable with to cross that color line?

5. NET assignment: Look up the lyrics to "Miss Otis Regrets." (You can even download it as a ringtone, as of this date.) Listen to several versions on YouTube, especially the ones by Bette Midler and Ella Fitzgerald. How does listening to the song influence your response to the essay? Which version do you like better, and why?

Signatures

1. Wanzer, an African American woman, is clearly self-conscious being in the "whitebready" club. Have there been any instances when you have been uncomfortable in a social setting? Why or why not?

2. Wanzer makes a point of identifying the ethnicity of the people serving or entertaining. In doing this, is she guilty of being biased herself? Or might there be some justification to her labeling?

3. What is going on in the exchange between the pianist and narrator? Does the exchange support the essay? And what about the friendship between Wanzer and Camille? Should Camille be oblivious to her friend's discomfort?

4. NET assignment: Who is Michel Foucault? Research his philosophy on "the order of things." How does this work for Wanzer's opening and closing?

Winter Seagull

1. Music and literature are both binding cultural forces. How does music and poetry figure in this essay in relation to the two Japanese families and to Washizu and the barber?

2. Washizu becomes a sort of bridge between two cultures, a willing eyewitness to a tragic scene, because of his shared ethnicity and ability to translate. Have you or anyone you have known had to translate for family or friends? And do you believe that you should speak the native language of the country you live in?

3. AIDS was a term much feared in the eighties and nineties. Has that fear faded in the United States or in your country? Yes or no? Explore the reasons behind your answer.

4. Homophobia is nonexistent in some cultures, rampant in others. What clues can you find regarding the cultural beliefs toward homosexuality in Japanese culture? What are the ramifications of these beliefs, in this case?

5. NET assignment: Japan is a culture of many rituals. Research either the Japanese tea ceremony, the ritual of *seppuku* or *harakiri* (suicide), or the funeral/death ritual. How do your findings add depth to this story?

Itam

1. What evidence of the crossing over of cultures can you find in this essay? Do you believe each culture develops on its own, or is culture influenced by others? Cite examples.

2. Consider the lifestyle of the Uyghurs. Does anything about it surprise you?

3. Being a Peace Corps volunteer in foreign territory has its challenges. Could you be a Peace Corps volunteer? Why or why not? If so, where would you hope to travel to, and why? Could you live in standards not up to what you are used to every day?

4. The Peace Corps was founded in 1961 by former U.S. president John F. Kennedy. What was his motivation to drum up a core of volunteers? Why do you suppose U.S. volunteerism is down today, relative to where it was in the 1960s?

5. NET assignment: Research the greetings in different cultures, including the Uyghur greeting. What leads to these differences? What impact might learning the greetings of host countries have when tourists visit?

High Tech in Gaborone

1. This essay begins with a strong opening line about technology and nature. How does the rest of the essay support Bauman's thesis? Give concrete examples from this essay and from outside world examples.

2. How does Ed's character makeup fit with the type of work he is doing? Do you think he belongs where he is, at least for the time being?

3. The essay has a humorous tone, and foreigners will laugh at the lawn mower stories. But should we? Does our laughter imply a sense of superiority, or a sense of shared humanity?

4. On p. 115, Bauman describes Ed's photos as "a fable in miniature." How does the tone and style of the essay lend itself to a fable?

5. NET assignment: Research the country of Kanye, Africa. What can you find on its growing tourism or water issues? How does what you find relate to this essay?

Triptych: Paradise

1. Wright relays the local marrying customs on p. 122. Every culture has its own marriage rituals, which generally have a practical, social reason behind them. What might the social reason be behind the customs in Santa Maria de Jesús?

2. Discuss the history of the chicken buses. Did you know the United States sent its old buses to other countries? What do you think of Guatemala's adaptation to the yellow buses, and the implications of having to colorize them?

3. On p. 127, Wright reveals the problem of pesticides and worker conditions. We have unions in the United States to protect workers' rights, but many resent unions for the problems they believe they cause. Given the conditions that can exist without them, do you feel unions are a positive or negative force in U.S. culture?

4. Wright refers several times to the wind over Lake Atitlán, which has an unsettling effect on tourists. How does this lead to the last line, "We are always a little bit afraid"? Do you live that way in your community? Why or why not?

5. NET assignment: Look up the Guatemalan civil war. What were the guerillas fighting for? What is the situation today?

Assailing Otherness

1. "Places are best soaked in through the tongue." Do you agree with Grigg-Saito's statement? Does her essay prove her thesis?

2. Consider how diet is cultural. Food rituals and habits vary from country to country, and Grigg-Saito notes religion is often the basis of these rules. This serves to provide a connection with a culture, but what happens when we face another culture's food practice?

3. How did you feel while reading this essay? Do your own cultural beliefs make you "curl up your nose"? Or is this something that you would try to eat?

4. Grigg-Saito is of mixed descent. She explores being the "other." Does this word take on positive or negative connotations in her explorations? What do you think society should work at to eradicate otherness?

5. NET assignment: Find recipes for unusual dishes that include ingredients such as insects, which are growing in popularity as a food staple (see the following essay, "Fried Locusts," by Kamela Jordan). Connect them to their parent cultures, and theorize why that culture might have developed that meal.

Fried Locusts

1. On p. 148, Jordan describes an early incident in their school in which she runs away from the fact that she can't understand Thai language. Can you imagine going to school in an environment where you can't understand your teacher or classmates? How do you think you would handle such a situation? And if you have had this experience, how did you handle it?

2. On p. 151, Jordan repeats some racial taunts. One refers to Negroes. What do you make of Thai children using harmful words and songs? And of Jordan's statement: "even in the most isolated valley, every child knows the song"?

3. If you don't read this essay carefully, you could be left with the impression that it's a simple, lyrical, often amusing recounting of a young girl's idyllic childhood in Thailand, and of exotic Thai "food snacks." But on closer reading, what pokes through?

4. NET assignment: Plug "Thai names" into your search engine and see what comes up. Note the names of Jordan's peers. Explore the Thai custom of naming, and what their naming tradition might say about Thai society.

Israel: Devour the Darling Plagues

1. Morris explains the symbolism of food. Consider foods in your own culture that might have historical significance. Do the names or preparations have any added symbolism?

2. Explore different attitudes in various cultures toward food and entertaining guests. How might it differ? Be similar? And what could the traditions signify?

3. Advertising reveals much about a culture. View some ads on television, or in magazines. What do the ads reflect about your customs, beliefs, and societal expectations?

4. Morris juxtaposes Israeli attitudes toward dieting in 1981 versus 2011. How has the U.S. culture affected Israeli women? Is it a positive or negative effect? What are the dietary attitudes in your own country?

5. NET assignment: Search the terms "The Pesach seder" and "Moses and the Ten Plagues." Now read Morris's introduction again within the historical context. How does it strike you, the pairing of candy and such a violent background within such a joyous celebration as this seder?

Connections

1. How important is friendship in your life? Would you be able to live at "the end of nowhere"? What would you gain? What would you lose? Does the U.S. culture (or your own culture) demand we be actively social?

2. See the paragraph on p. 167. Much is said here about Goddard's emotional makeup, and her need for space. Do you think your social environment growing up dictates how you will live life later? If your answer is yes, how so? If no, why not?

3. What do you think of Goddard's six examples of connection? What words keep cropping up that gives clues to her "needs"?

4. NET assignment: Do a search for the term "hermit." What can you find about the word and the history and attitudes

toward hermits? Would it surprise you to find out that many of the women and men accused of witchery during the witch hysteria were hermits? What parts of the hermetic lifestyle might lead to a society's condemnation of them and make them more vulnerable?

Palo del Muerte

1. Simmons lives near the Mexican border. How might his beliefs be formed by this borderland culture and environment, and by the teachings of his mother, a Swedish immigrant?

2. Buntin's religious quest and beliefs differ in part from those of his wife. Why? Do you believe that people who don't have religious beliefs have more trouble feeling like they belong or are part of something than those who do?

3. What accounts for religious extremism or religious dogma when so many cultures hold differing beliefs? What are your beliefs, and did anyone in your family guide you to them? What effect do you think the Internet might have on the future of dogmatic beliefs?

4. Buntin eventually settles on a rather pantheistic, polyreligious view of God. How does the *palo del muerte* tree symbolize this for him? What needs are answered by his current beliefs? And what leads him to finally find his way?

5. NET assignment: Research the history of angel sightings. How and when do they appear? Do you believe in them? And what about your *personal religion* makes you have this opinion? Can you accept possibilities, or do you need black and white answers? Finally, how does your *cultural* background influence this belief or nonbelief in angels?

INTERCULTURAL CONNECTIONS

These are simple connections to jumpstart discussion between the connecting essays in order to increase the awareness of each topic. You may find your own connections between these essays, and we encourage you to explore all of them in juxtaposition.

1. **Autman and Wright**: first impressions of airports and a new place; cultural changes in religious icons such as the Book of Mormon and the church doors at the Cathedral of San José.

2. **Jordan and Wright**: hint at underlying danger and civil unrest.

3. **Grigg-Saito, Jordan, and Morris**: the cultural significance and experience of foreign food.

4. **Lovett, Bauman, and Hayes-Raitt**: the importance of photographs in finding identity and sharing community.

5. **Autman, Parker, and Wanzer**: racism and stereotyping.

6. **Bauman and Goddard**: characters who live outside of their childhood community in some manner.

7. **Sartwell and Klebenov Jacobs**: family history through letters; the mix of two distinct religious backgrounds and ethnicities.

8. **Bannwart ("Tightrope") and Washizu**: art as a tool to bridge gaps.

9. **Sartwell and Stark**: issues of being the "other."

10. **Goddard and Buntin**: exploration of internal landscape that reflects their outer landscape.

11. **Stark and Buntin**: the cultural significance of visions.

12. **Autman and Buntin**: the search for a spiritual self.

13. **Stoner and Jordan**: Third Culture Kids.

14. **Stoner and Stark**: the concept of "home" when one is constantly moving.

15. **Hayes-Raitt and Bannwart ("Reflecting")**: war through, and in, the eyes of a child.

QUOTATIONS EXPLORATION

Explore each quotation found on the part openers in context with the accompanying part essays.

ABOUT THE EDITOR

Tara L. Masih received a BA in English and a minor in sociology from C. W. Post College, along with an MA in Writing and Publishing from Emerson College (where she taught Freshman Composition and Grammar). She is editor of the award-winning *Rose Metal Press Field Guide to Writing Flash Fiction* (2009), and author of the story collection *Where the Dog Star Never Glows* (2010), which *Publishers Weekly* described as "striking and resonant." Masih has published in numerous anthologies and literary magazines (such as *Confrontation, Hayden's Ferry Review, Natural Bridge, The Los Angeles Review,* and *The Caribbean Writer*), and her essays have been read on NPR and anthologized in numerous textbooks.

Awards for her work include first place in *The Ledge Magazine*'s fiction contest, a finalist fiction grant from the Massachusetts Cultural Council, and Pushcart Prize, *Best New American Voices,* and Best of the Web nominations. She judges the Intercultural Essay prize for the annual Soul-Making Keats Literary Contest.

Masih was a regular contributor to *The Indian-American* and *Masala* magazines, where her essays on race and culture were often featured. She now works as a freelance book editor in Andover, Massachusetts, and teaches part time at Grub Street, in Boston. You can find her at www.taramasih.com and on Goodreads and Facebook.

MICHAEL GILLIGAN

ACKNOWLEDGMENTS

First and foremost, I can't thank my publisher enough—Nancy Cleary believed in this book, even during tough economic times; she was a joy to work with, created a stunning cover and interior design, and understood all the sensitivities of this project. Thanks also to Eileen Malone, Director of the Soul-Making Keats Literary Contest. Every year she works hard to give a voice to other writers with her boundless enthusiasm and support. David Mura gets my sincere gratitude for finding time in his busy schedule to introduce this collection and grace us with his insightful and poetic thoughts, and Dr. Zaline M. Roy-Campbell stepped in during a busy time as well to review the questions and adeptly fine-tune them. Thanks go to my contributors, talented writers and artists who shared their deepest thoughts and keenest observations as well as their travel and family photos. Finally, thanks to blurbers Faith Adiele, Robert Olen Butler, Diane Glancy, Suzanne Kamata, and Mary M. Slechta; I respect all of you in your roles as writers, editors, and teachers who have worked to broaden intercultural understanding.

—Tara L. Masih

ABOUT THE
INTRODUCTION AUTHOR

David Mura is a poet, creative nonfiction and fiction writer, critic, playwright, and performance artist. A Sansei, or third-generation Japanese American, Mura has written two memoirs: *Turning Japanese: Memoirs of a Sansei*, which won a 1991 Josephine Miles Book Award from the Oakland PEN and was listed as a *New York Times* Notable Book of the Year; and *Where the Body Meets Memory: An Odyssey of Race, Sexuality and Identity* (1996). His most recent work is the novel *Famous Suicides of the Japanese Empire* (2008), a finalist for the Minnesota Book Award, the John Gardner Fiction Prize, and the Virginia Commonwealth University Cabell First Novelist Award.

Mura's award-winning poetry books include *Angels for the Burning* (2004), *The Colors of Desire* (1995), and *After We Lost Our Way* (1989). His critical essays, *Song for Uncle Tom, Tonto, & Mr. Moto: Poetry & Identity*, were published in the University of Michigan Press's Poets on Poetry series (2002).

Along with African American writer Alexs Pate, Mura created and performs a multimedia performance piece, *Secret Colors*, about their lives as men of color and Asian American–African American relations. A film adaptation, titled *Slowly, This*, was broadcast in the PBS series *ALIVE TV*. Mura has also been featured on the Bill Moyers PBS series *The Language of Life*.

Mura helped found and served as the artistic director for the Asian American Renaissance and is on the advisory board of VONA, a writers' conference for writers of color. He currently teaches in the Stonecoast MFA Program at the University of Southern Maine. You can find him at www.davidmura.com.

INDEX OF CONTRIBUTORS